The Road To Me

The Road To Me

✦

Reclaiming Your Power

Gary W. Richman, Ph.D.

iUniverse, Inc.
New York   Bloomington

The Road To Me

Reclaiming Your Power

iUniverse books may be ordered through booksellers or by contacting:

iUniverse
1663 Liberty Drive
Bloomington, IN 47403
www.iuniverse.com
1-800-Authors (1-800-288-4677)

Because of the dynamic nature of the Internet, any Web addresses or links contained in this book may have changed since publication and may no longer be valid. The views expressed in this work are solely those of the author and do not necessarily reflect the views of the publisher, and the publisher hereby disclaims any responsibility for them.

ISBN: 978-0-595-50861-7 (pbk)
ISBN: 978-0-595-61680-0 (ebk)

Printed in the United States of America

To all those who courageously do their inner personal work pursuing their own deepest and truest essence of self.

Contents

Acknowledgements

To Ann West, Earl Strompell, and Gretchen Kvistad for their efforts to help formulate, edit, and hone the early workings and examples for this book. To Robin Anderson for her editing, facilitating, and managing of my work. I am truly grateful to you all. To others who have always been there with support and unconditional love: Paul and Nanette Holland, Bruce Orinstein, Laura Torrence, Miriam Haines, Lon Orenstein, Bonnie Miller, Richard and Jody Kornblath, Robin Kunysz, Rick Moss, and Amy Roth.

To my wife, Lisa, who is my treasure and my joy.

Introduction

The Road To Me: Reclaiming Your Power puts into plain language a way of understanding psychotherapy as a method of undoing the "learned" sense of self in order to embrace our own true self. It is meant to help you "get out of your own way" so that you can reclaim and actualize your personal power. It offers a path for helping individuals to heal and to become better acquainted with themselves. It is a precursor to embracing one's soul. To become aware of the soul is to touch those parts of ourselves that house the higher self—the essence within. It is this underlying component of the self from which all true wholeness and oneness evolve.

The Road To Me is the process by which one begins to access the higher self, one's essence within. We all have to work out and develop muscles that allow us to be in better physical shape. Everyone is familiar with physical working out and the benefits. No one has to tell you about this, but we don't think of our emotional fitness as an essential part of our consciousness with regard to our health and well-being.

The emotional workout focuses inside. It is doing the insight-oriented work to understand and reinterpret the dark shadow of our own limitations and fears. The more we begin to stretch, to be more conscious and introspective the more we are engaging our truth. Truth is the inner barometer available to everyone that accesses it, never lies or misdirects us. Therefore, just like beginning to get into physical shape, inner directing your intention/attention is the first step to being in emotional shape. As we emotionally workout, usually with the help of a professional facilitator (in the physical workout world this professional is called a trainer and there is no embarrassment with employing this type of help) we move toward our inner essence developing a stronger and more empowered self. The result of continuing your emotional workout is strengthening the inner muscles of strength and power that enhance self-esteem and confidence.

Many people cannot imagine themselves as any different or any more than they already are. They believe that who they have known themselves to be is all they can be. If, for example, you have always known yourself to be passive, unlucky, or not loveable, you may then believe you will always be these things. Based on your past, what else could you believe? How could your personal reality be any different? In the same way we believe that it would be too hard to have the body we want even with physically working out, the same holds true when we commence our emotional workout. It is hard to imagine the end results when we have not been there before.

Our sense of self is a concept we have learned. It is our experience. However, higher knowledge has proven that a concept is not a constant. Before Einstein, scientists thought the Newtonian atom was all the atomic reality that existed. Today we know that the atom is only a shell of what we currently call atomic reality. Likewise, the "learned personality," which most people believe is the reality of who they truly are and will remain, is only the shell in which our true essence lies.

The "learned personality" is the part of us that constantly needed to accommodate the family system in which we were raised. Each of us had to do certain things and behave in certain ways in order to be considered good card-carrying members of our own families. A child cannot just pack a bag and hit the streets at five years old, although a client of mine tried to do this very thing. He gathered his treasures and walked through the kitchen because he wanted to impress upon his family how bad it was for him to be there. To his horror, his parents just laughed at the cute antics of their child. Dismayed, he returned to his room, unpacked his bag, and cried. Like all children, he knew he could not survive alone. His attempt had been an empty gesture. He had to adjust to his lot and learn to get whatever warmth and love he could from his parents. And like all of us, he had to learn to suppress his own "little one," his personal power, his essence, his soul, in order to survive and to be accepted.

Of course, because this situation occurs unconsciously and very early on in life, our "little one," whom we have learned to hold in disdain, usually goes so far under cover that this part of us becomes virtually undetectable. Very few people retain an awareness of their true inner self beyond an occasional glimpse of it, as though they were seeing an illusion pop up over the horizon just before it sinks back out of sight. Even such a fleeting glance gets written off as a grandiose moment, impossible to capture. It is analogous to grasping at a dream experienced in the night, something out of one's reach.

However, we can access a shift in consciousness that makes it possible to unlearn the defined self. As a friend said to me, "It's not that seeing is believing, but believing is seeing." It sounds so simple, doesn't it? And once we get our neurotic selves out of the way, it is simple! This book is a guide to the unlearning of the "learned personality." It addresses the steps to healing the self, followed by the care taking of the shell of the ego, and ultimately realizing the underlying spirit within.

Upon beginning therapy, many of my clients express a feeling of hopelessness. They wonder how they can unlearn what they have always identified as themselves in order to find the essence of the soulful self. We begin by discussing the courage it will take to deal with the complex work ahead, and the fact that this can be frightening. This is parallel to beginning any workout that challenges us. We must develop new and consistent habits and disciplines if we are to get the desired results (and unlearn those bad habits which no longer serve us).

Most often, initial therapy sessions expose a gut-level fear in clients that what they have been brought up to believe about themselves is in fact true. And worst of all, they believe their "little one" hiding inside is really an awful, unworthy child no one could ever like and certainly no one could love. Since this is a bottom-line feeling, it is frightening to go inside the psyche where a dark, unacceptable side of themselves may loom. It is my belief that this fear is the reason so many people criticize therapy and avoid doing their own work. They would rather keep their shadow self at arms length, running from it rather than confronting it.

In our culture, men are more prone than women to flee from their deepest feelings. Under the guise of "being a man," very few of us have learned to deal with this part of the self. I often tell male clients that it seems easier not to deal with issues than it is to confront our emotions. Walking away is initially much easier than facing one's self. But in the long run, walking away often leads to another, more difficult road.

There is a misconception many hold about the way to override the shadow side of the personality. Many choose the path of least resistance by not confronting their dark side, retaining some semblance of hope that their good deeds will one day virtually chase away their dread of being unworthy. However, the typical reason people begin to explore their lives more deeply is that this approach is not working. Our shadow side seems to show up repeatedly and unexpectedly, even when we think it is under control.

To commence one's emotional fitness workout means having to look at repetitive patterns that get you in trouble and sabotage your life. But I want to comfort those who imagine an inner self that is irretrievably damaged. I assure you this work will only reveal a wonderful person whose wounds we can heal. Although you may believe the reality of your personality and the shadow self, I know that in the long run, as we do the work, you will find what I say to be true.

So why do we call all of this work? Because it is often a difficult, taxing process that leaves one feeling frustrated and fatigued. But the process can also be enjoyable because you are discovering patterns that have caused you to suffer. Therefore, you get to see progress, which offers a great sense of personal gratification, as well as ongoing glimpses of your actualized self. But all of this is a choice one makes and there are no free lunches. If you want beneficial results, you have to reach for them, and this takes time.

Even with computers, fax machines, modems, air travel, phones, and modern technology, emotions still take the same amount of time to be felt and healed. Our voices and thoughts can move faster because they are part of the intellect. Our emotions are part of the unconscious, the heart, and they cannot be rushed. Heart messages come from that inner place of the intangible. Such communication is not about thought, logic, or deductive reasoning. You cannot convince your heart that it should be stronger or understand why it is experiencing fear. It must feel protected in order to approach what it considers dangerous emotional territory. Until that feeling of safety occurs, nothing on earth will convince the heart to move out of the shadows.

The important thing in life is to go for it. Quantum physics suggests that the movement of matter has a self-prophesying aspect as it shifts in the direction of expectations. When we seize our destiny and have the intention of becoming more, energy is released to facilitate our end goal. The more we focus on the intention we have for our lives the more we receive just what we ask for.

This book outlines a tangible and easily followed path to your true self. It describes the importance of doing internal work to achieve peace, joy, and abundance. By acquiring the terms and direction for the unlearning of our learned personality, we can realize the power of being true to what lies within. *The Road To Me: Reclaiming Your Power* offers a definitive path to success for anyone who has the courage to walk into the essence/truth within, make friends with it, and be empowered by it.

Section I

The Process: Self

✦

1

Beginning the Work

✦

Understanding The Learned Personality

We live in a world in which a commonly used phrase is "Don't fix it if it isn't broken." Unfortunately, we often apply this same sentiment to our mental and physical health. Insurance companies support this mentality, keeping a stranglehold on our ability to get preventative, if not complete medical or mental health care. Our culture is handcuffed to the dictate of waiting until we are obviously "broken" before we are "fixed." And, to make matters worse, our need to be macho makes us feel like wimps if we ask for help before we are at death's door or our mental health has deteriorated to a point that we are clinically depressed or suicidal. With such dogma firmly entrenched in our thoughts, it is not surprising that those who seek psychotherapy do so because they, their partners, or their families are already breaking down or broken. When these people finally decide to go to therapy, sessions are often seen as a last ditch effort to reestablish equilibrium. Most people do not wait for a negative diagnosis from a physician before they physically workout, why do they do that with their emotional health? And how many get help with their emotional state only for as long as it takes for the pain to go away? Is that how you would run your physical workouts? As soon as your heart rate and muscle tone are better you terminate your workouts? Of course not.

Sometimes people go to therapy just to be able to say that they did everything possible to get their relationship back on track before finally leaving a marriage or partnership. Initially, clients may not think in terms

3

of how they can prevent a problem from happening again, mostly they just want uncomfortable feelings to go away. And, most individuals do not expect to work hard to enhance their relationships. In fact, some would consider it a plus to find the other person at fault. Insurance companies further reinforce these attitudes by supporting only the time needed to accomplish quick "fix it" goals. And so we are left with an assembly line mentality, perpetuating the impression that therapists can simply turn a couple of bolts, patch what is not working, and usher people back to their lives. Yet the life people return to, the "old life," is usually the very root of the problem, and will again fan the flames of discomfort and discontent.

Another rule of our society is "He who dies with the most toys wins." With this as our banner of success, many of us define ourselves solely by materialistic validation—the size and location of our home, the price or make of our car, the labels in our clothes, the ratings of the restaurants we frequent, or the variety of unneeded luxuries we have acquired. Recently, a client told me that he and his wife had just bought a mansion in a prestigious neighborhood. He said that after seeing the house, a friend commented that the man had finally "arrived." Clearly, it was not personal growth or wisdom that served as the barometer of his upgraded position in his friend's eyes.

Have you ever noticed that people rarely ask who you are? The inquiry is more often about what you do. Even if there are no questions asked, new acquaintances are probably waiting to see what your business card says. This is a big part of the reason so many men, and some women, come to my office in deep pain around the time of a mid-life crisis. They have the appropriate spouse, two children in private school, a big house, a boat or a plane, fancy cars, a summer home, and a country club membership, but still they feel lonely and empty. The work is the same for all of them—moving away from defining themselves by material possessions and moving toward regaining their empowered selves.

The quest for authenticity to shift from what is outside to what is inside seems a common process to those of us in the west who have lost the meaning of the "who" in who we are. We have forgotten the perennial wisdom in the old television series Kung Fu. In the show, Cane, the main character, is constantly asked what he is. His response is always the same: "I am a man." Although the answer may seem a matter of mere semantics, it points to the essence of identifying ourselves with our inner truth. Many of us have become so caught up in materialism that we mistakenly believe our possessions reflect our true self.

Recently, one of my clients was deciding whether or not to buy a Porsche, and I was trying to understand his motives. If he were buying the car because he could afford it, because of its great handling and because it would give him pleasure to drive, then I thought he should buy the car. But if he was buying the car as an extension or an enhancement of his esteem, then I wanted to direct him to reexamine his motives. Thus, the search for the inner self is made more potent by the thoughtful, guided work we do in therapy, free from the distractions that typically keep us from a deeper sense of who we are.

Emotional and spiritual emptiness begin in our early years, at a time in our lives when we are easily influenced by people who subscribe to the "my toys are me" theory. The Bible says that the children "shall inherit the sins of their father's." This might instead read that the children shall inherit the compulsions and anxieties of their parents. When parents are not aware of their emotional baggage, societal or familial, they will undoubtedly model and pass on their personal neuroses to their children. What a shock to reach mid-life only to discover that, even after carefully following society's road map, you are not whole, centered, or happy. And the sense of being overwhelmed is accentuated when people realize the tradeoffs—headaches and backaches, escalating stress, and multiple physiological disorders. Imagine the dismay of my clients when I tell them that despite years of working to build a "successful life" the hardest work is still ahead of them.

The good news is that because of their hard work over the course of time, many people seeking therapy have already developed the wherewithal to engage in the necessary inner work. And, although they have been behaving in certain ways for a long time, it will take less time to unlearn this painful and empty existence than it did to create it. In order to begin however, one must understand the origins of the self and how and why the learned personality came into existence.

Many people in mid-life do not want to believe they need to focus on the origins of their personality in psychotherapy. They feel confident that they have gotten over or moved beyond whatever was going on in their "early years." But, while the idea of moving on is great, it takes a lot more than a simple "get over it" statement in order to truly move forward in one's life.

Dr. R. D. Lang, a well-known English psychiatrist, wrote that we are the sum total of our experiences. We do not grow up in a vacuum; we evolve from the roots of our beginning. Psychology literature states that who we are and how we believe others see us is indelibly written by the age of eight. Thus, Freud and others realize that the unconscious is a powerful creator and mover of an individual's personality. If we do not unlearn the negative, hidden aspects of this learned personality, we will continually be amazed by its control over us.

Before you object to this perspective, ask yourself this: When was the last time you involved yourself in a behavior or in a type of relationship you were certain you would never again exhibit or become involved in? Weren't you dead sure you had this figured out and could spot the situation that might tempt you to repeat your mistakes? The problem is that even if you have a conscious sense of the external problem, you probably do not have a conscious sense of what is going on inside of you that makes you create the problem in the first place. There is a reason that this level is called the unconscious. It is beyond consciousness.

When a child is born, its whole purpose is to survive. Every aspect of an infant's being interacts with primitive instinctual forces. In order to thrive, its physical needs must be met. Food, sleep, protection from harm, and shelter are essential for survival. A child's emotional well being is also essential; being supported, touched, held, and made to feel warm, loved, and safe.

In 1965, Dr. Harry Harlow at the University of Wisconsin did a famous study with Rhesus monkeys. He took a wire figure of a mother monkey and fastened to it a bottle of milk with the nipple protruding where the breast should be. Dr. Harlow assembled another wire figure and bottle setup, this time wrapping it completely in cloth. Baby monkeys nursed from one or the other of the figures for the duration of the study, and some nursed on both. The results were twofold. First, the baby monkeys preferred the cloth wrapped surrogate mother. And second, the babies who had exposure only to the wire surrogate did not thrive as well as those who nursed from the cloth monkey. In addition, Dr. Harlow found that later in life the baby monkeys who had nursed only on the unwrapped wire figure, and survived, were not able to fit in or act appropriately when introduced into adult social and sexual situations. Based on these findings, it was his contention that babies need more than food and water. Thus, the enhancement of the being is not solely based on material sustenance but also on the nurturing and feeding of the inner self, initially through the warmth and contact of touch.

It is the feeling state, or what romantically may be called the "heart," that leads the way to our empowerment. Within the heart is our essence, our true nature, strength, feelings, and potential. I believe that all of our potential is present from the moment we plop onto this plane of existence. Yet, during infancy our physical being must first and foremost learn to survive. We assess intuitively how to get our needs met from primary caregivers, usually our biological parents. And the learned personality or ego begins to take shape as we conform ourselves to those who take care of our needs.

Soul, Essence & Personality

Many of you may wonder what the distinction is between the soul, the essence, and the personality. It is important to recognize these as three distinct concepts. One way to understand this is with the image of a hierarchical grid. First, the part of us that observes and consults from a higher plane (sometimes referred to as our higher self) is what I believe is the soul. This is the energy described by quantum physics, metaphysics, and spiritual terminology, and is the upper end of the grid, the realm in which all of us aspire to connect. Second, the essence of an individual is that which exists at the core of a complete person. This is the true collaboration of both intellect and instinct, and can be achieved once our neurotic baggage is out of the way. In Eastern religion this center is described as the seat of individual power, or the most authentic sense of self. It is the inner state we strive for in life. It is what we glimpse when we are at our best. Most psychotherapeutic, metaphysical, and spiritual goals emphasize how to realize this essence, bringing about an awareness that ensures personal fulfillment. The third and lowest level of the grid is the learned personality. Remember, this is the way we think of ourselves after we've accommodated and conformed to our unique family system. It is the most visible component of who we have experienced ourselves to be. The good news is that what is learned can be unlearned.

The personality develops from the unconscious, so this is where we will begin. The word "unconscious" may mean very little to you except that it has something to do with childhood. Psychotherapists use this term to indicate what may be running us without our being in control. It is simply that which is not conscious. Now you may be thinking, "He has a Ph.D. and this is what he comes up with?" Well, yes. However, keep reading to see the amazing way the unconscious unfolds, its function, and how it controls your life more than any conscious, experiential, or mature thought you may have.

From birth to about eight years of age, a child relates mostly from affective states, more commonly known as feelings. For example, most of what children take in, and how they interpret their world, is perceived emotionally. If you have been around children, you know that they do not demonstrate logical, deductive reasoning until they are between nine and eleven years old. Instead, early perceptions with a feeling base underlie a child's reality regarding survival, life and death survival as they experience it. This collection of feelings and perceptions is what makes up the unconscious.

The survival language of the unconscious is based on all or nothing questions about how we feel. Am I protected or vulnerable? Do I feel included or excluded? Do I feel appreciated or unappreciated? Do I feel accepted or rejected? Do I feel loved or unloved? These subtle perceptions sum up a child's sense of self-identity and define the surrounding world.

From early impressions, infants and toddlers begin to display two underlying paradigms of the unconscious; self-identity and world-identity. Self-identity is the inner most sense, at an almost cellular level, of who one knows oneself to be. World identity is the innermost feeling of what can be expected from the world and how it will relate to us. The more a child must suppress his or her essence, the more erroneous perceptions of reality will build in the unconscious. In this way, children become victims of their parent's system. It follows that the healthier the parents are the less victimized the child is. Nevertheless, any victimization gets logged in the unconscious and becomes a mistaken definition of the self and the world.

We can conclude that children process naturally from a narcissistic orientation. This common psychological term originated in Greek mythology. Narcissus was a character in Greek mythology that spent his time looking into a pool of water, gazing at his own reflection. Those diagnosed as narcissistic, when looking out into the world, seem to see only their own reflection. They have self-centered pictures that mirror the world in the exact way they want it to be, rather than as it is. Infants and toddlers are naturally and primarily narcissistic. In other words, if they are hungry, they are fed; if they are wet, they are changed; if they are frightened, they are comforted, and so on. Thus, they naturally see themselves as the center of the Universe.

When a parent does not respond as the child expects, children may feel they have done something wrong. This has serious effects. First, they may fear they will not, in an all or nothing fashion, be loved. And, they experience a sense of rejection that is inharmonious with their innate sense of survival. Therefore, they do what is necessary to get back in line with the world so it will react to them as they expect. They also revamp their view of themselves and the world in the process so as not to jeopardize their safety, which hinges entirely on being accepted by their caregivers.

What is important when dealing with safety is whether or not the child feels (not thinks) he or she is a full card carrying member of the family. Children understand that they must accommodate to their particular home system in order to maintain their good standing, in order to survive. But this pursuit is neither conscious nor intellectual. From a gut level, children continually hope their environment will offer the mechanisms and tools necessary for them to thrive. This hope is kept alive at any cost, and most often the cost is the child's own self worth.

The second aspect of the unconscious process is to automatically blame oneself. This is related to the fact that children, like all infant creatures, have an inherent bond to their parents. Unconsciously, this is translated as: My primary caregivers are god-like beings who are here for my survival and betterment. These god-like beings are created by my design because I need them to be all knowing, all-powerful, and truly altruistic. Therefore, all I need to do is to absorb everything. Remember, this is an innate not logical assumption or design on the part of the child.

What happens then if one's primary caregivers do not provide what is needed? If these gods have it to give but don't give it, then it appears to the child that they themselves do not deserve these gifts they so desperately need. Self-blame is all encompassing and becomes logged into a child's sense of self worth. There is no one on duty to explain that what is being asked for is appropriate and fair. There is no one to explain that the parents may be limited or psychologically wounded and unable to give what is needed or wanted. The blame simply shifts to the self.

For example, if a child wants a hug or some kind of nurturing and does not receive it, she might believe her request has been asked for incorrectly. If another attempt is made with no positive outcome, again she believes she is not doing it right. There are two reasons for this. The first, as mentioned above, relates to primary narcissism. The second relates to the component of hope. For the child to continue, she must have hope that her parents can give her what she needs. Without hope, any child will automatically and understandably fail to thrive. I often tell my clients that if they had figured out how dysfunctional their parents were they probably would have lost all hope. Without hope, depression would have set in, possibly giving way to future substance abuse and eventually suicidal thoughts or death. But by accepting self-blame and continually trying to get through to our parents, we allow hope to stay alive.

The negative internalization of incompetence by children in order to thrive is a consequence of their parent's unresolved issues. When, even through perseverance, a child can never get what he needs, a complete sense of failing is logged at the unconscious level. This negatively impacts the child's gut level sense of self-identity, and failure becomes a self-reality.

For example, those who grow up in an alcoholic or angry home have tremendous difficulty allowing goodness to remain in their lives for too long. As they experience happiness, they begin to feel some level of agitation. As the good feelings continue to rise, so does the sense of agitation. At some point, as good as good might feel, the heightened agitation accompanying good feelings becomes so uncomfortable that the person sabotages his or her own happiness in order to diminish the agitation.

This happens because in dysfunctional homes, one never knows what kind of situation to expect. A child might come home with exciting news, but there may be chaos going on that disrupts the good feelings. If this continues, the child learns over time that happiness cannot be trusted and, at best, will not last or will be taken away. The unconscious inherits the following perception: The self is not worthy of happiness and the world is not a place that allows sustained goodness.

When we take a damaged unconscious into adulthood, we reap the self-fulfilling prophecy of our beliefs about reality. Deep down we believe the world cannot respond to us in just any old particular way. Thus, our innermost sense refuses the idea that our destiny can be whatever we want. It insists that we have only that which we have "learned" is our due. And to make matters worse, the unconscious is like radar that draws to us only that which we inwardly believe is our right. Therefore, if you were molested or beaten as a child, your unconscious brings those who will oblige your sense of victimization into your life. This is why we hear of women who stay with husbands who beat them. If one feels destined to be abused, and unconsciously expects to go from one abusive relationship to the next, why leave the abusive person you are in a relationship with? What would be the point?

And so, I often work with people who realize they've again ended up in the same stuck place in their life. Even though they understand what they keep doing, they have been unable to break the pattern. This is because the timeless unconscious does not significantly change with age or maturity. Whatever it has logged as being crucial for survival, it will continue to pursue. Above all, this learned internalization must be unlearned at the same feeling level from which it was created, the cellular core of one being. Though there are many ways to do this, the way I believe in and the vehicle I have seen work most successfully is psychotherapy.

The learned personality is the sense of "who I am and how I expect the world will relate to me" based on internalization in the unconscious of early experiences and interactions with our primary caregivers. That is, the learned personality is the way we believe we must be because of consistently reinforced life experiences. In actuality, our manner of "being" is merely a manifestation of our primary learning, fed into our unconscious computer during our upbringing. In psychology, these are the continual behavior patterns that originate in our unconscious and that we redundantly play out in our lives. In psychology, these are called repetition compulsions.

Unfortunately, once we have in place a false identification of our sense of self and the way the world is, we take that on the road. We interact with others, behaving from our learned sense of who we imagine ourselves to be. The more we continue this pattern the more we truly believe this is who we are. When I ask clients how long they remember feeling a certain way, they typically say, "for as long as I can remember." However, once they grasp the concept of learned behavior they begin to recall the negative patterns of past incidents still at play in their current life.

Each time we made an accommodation to our family system, whether for reasons of basic experience or because of punishment, we took another step toward suppressing our little one. And now, as we change beliefs about ourselves, our reality will also change. As our views change, the world begins to accommodate to the way we see it. It is at this point that deeper understanding of the learned personality and its effect on adulthood can really be brought to light.

Where the Heart is

The feeling we get as we grow up in our Western world is that the ego, our sense of self, is validated from "outside" our true being. Only the results of our labor seem to convince others how successful, credible, powerful, and acceptable we are. Moreover, we derive our strongest sense of well-being and accomplishment from involvement in outside events. For example, our bodily containers and the material things we have reflect the learned personality, our unconsciously chosen barometer of how others will evaluate and include us.

It is understandable that adolescents, with all of their body, mind, chemical, and life changes, focus on peer acceptability and external image instead of on the essence within them. Adults should be more aware. Unfortunately, in our Hollywood-driven, go to the movies, modern-day-hero society, adults are often just as wrapped up in our containers, the physical form of consciousness, as are adolescents. This perpetuates a sense of the body as the ego, without much connection to our internal sense of self.

The path of wisdom is to embrace our feelings and our actions, fully learning from life's triumphs and consequences. Nevertheless, when inklings of reality begin to hit home, people come to my office and to the offices of other therapists, to reevaluate their idea of the quality of life. Once here, they begin to accept that the only things that are everlasting are the lessons learned and internalized. These are then added to the essential self.

The next question is how we can alter our focus and priorities. The answer is simple and has been given in countless sources from the Tao to the Bible. We must come from the place where the essence lives, the heart. It is through the heart that the doors open and we begin to bloom. Unfortunately, many people remain ignorant about the real game.

However obvious this may seem, doing it is complex. Our personal process, as religion, philosophy, and psychology tell us, must be from the inside out. Think about it. When you throw a pebble into the water, in which direction do the rings flow? To believe that happiness, contentment, completeness, and wholeness will come from materialism or worship of the physical body is to go against Mother Nature. Let having and owning be secondary as your rings of wholeness spread. Do the necessary work of unlearning what you have erroneously been taught to believe. Only this will center your self and bring you lasting joy.

The heart, where God-like feelings exist, is the center of human contact with the Universe. It has always been so and it will always be so! It is healing to project love and care into the world. Haven't we had enough of toxic aggressive beliefs that teach us to do onto others before they do onto us? Many believe we are a hard, cruel people who cannot be counted on for anything noble. Yet, in times of environmental or human tragedy, people quickly rally to offer a helping hand. When we realize how fine we really are, we will begin to act daily from that place, even if this begins simply within our own families. We will begin to "practice random acts of kindness and senseless acts of beauty."

The Work

The emotional work is done in order to help our true being remember what love and passion really mean. It is from actually loving and being passionate about others and life that a sense of wholeness can be realized. Now some will say, "Of course," while others will groan, "Oh, that bit again? Why doesn't this guy come up with something original?" My response is this: There are no original thoughts, only original approaches. The good answers are almost always the same because they are the essence of truth.

The work is about unlearning the ego and moving forward into the true self. Many Buddhist texts describe how a student may study for years and then out of frustration almost scream at the master, demanding the key to enlightenment. The master will then do something like bop the student on the head, and all of a sudden he gets it. The "getting it," once gotten, seems so simple when you realize you have fooled yourself all along with inappropriate expectations and preconceived ideas. Now is the time to undo these preconceived ideas, to clean out the cobwebs and open the old boxes in order to receive your own "ah ha" experience.

In psychotherapy, the process is one of sorting out your acquired internalized baggage. By doing this, the heart or the "little one" (Bradshaw's defined "inner child") can become more available to feelings. This allows more love, that which connects us deeply with others and with the Universe. Psychological and metaphysical texts say we must let go of neuroses, or the ego, in order to find the true self. For me, this process is done in two stages.

The first is to shore up the ego by getting rid of the baggage of the learned personality. Only then will a person will be strong enough to truly surrender, allowing the essence of the inner self to bloom.

So, let's back up and start to define some new terms. One word to reconsider is love. To me this means "heartfeltness," unconditional caring that lives in the soul. It is the sense one gets when holding a newborn baby or the reason the movies E.T. and Field of Dreams were such big hits. Love is the soulful experience of resonating with events so blissfully that every cell is passionately aware of joy. This swell of feeling in the heart is beyond guardedness or personal armor, it is where vulnerability is not considered a liability and your whole emotional and physical being is wonderfully alive.

We all have glimpses of this state, but many view it only at the movies or witness it during extremely personal events. One of the most touching examples of this feeling for me was near the time of my father's passing. My parents had been together all their adult lives. The expression with which my mother looked at my father as she stood by his failing body was one of total love and compassion. It was the most tender moment I have ever witnessed, and I feel blessed to have been present to observe it.

2

Strengthening the Ego

✦

Pushing Buttons

When life situations trigger our unconscious mechanisms, our buttons get pushed and we react impulsively, from the learned personality or the unconscious. Unresolved wounds can be set off without warning, by anyone, with merely a word or a gesture. We've all overreacted emotionally to those people and things that set us off, and these experiences usually end up in feelings of loss, sadness, deep regret, or remorse.

These unwelcome reactions are often triggered by people we hold in high esteem or consider important in our lives; people we care about. Usually, these highly involuntary responses occur even if we know better than to overreact. But we just can't seem to stop ourselves. Afterward, we generally wish we hadn't behaved the way we did and become extremely apologetic or even remorseful. Nevertheless, we retain our unconscious knee-jerk potential and experience the same reactions over and over again.

Each of us has emotional buttons. Once they are pushed, it's as if our conscious self takes a back seat while the unconscious moves into the driver's seat. We react from survival mode until our unconscious is satisfied that we are safe. The bottom line of our reaction is always fear. The ultimate fear in life is abandonment or death.

My father told me a story about coming home from the fighting after World War II. Having just returned from the war, he was sleeping in his old room in his parent's home. One morning while he was asleep, his mother tiptoed into his room to put something away. He remembers waking up with a start and immediately beginning to yell at her. She too was startled. As he became more oriented to his immediate surroundings he got a hold of himself and realized what had happened. He explained to his frightened mother that in war a tiptoe means someone is sneaking up on you. He had learned in battle that when his surroundings were too quiet was when his life was most likely in jeopardy. He asked her to walk in a normal way in a room where he was sleeping which, because of his recent conditioning, would mean he was safe. He had learned this behavior in only a few short years, but it was completely ingrained because it had been based on the greatest fear, the ultimate measure of survival—life or death.

Another dilemma people often face is how difficult it seems to be to allow goodness or success into their lives. In fact, there are many who were raised in alcoholic, explosive, argumentative, or very critical and judgmental homes in which peace and quiet could be severely disrupted at any time and without warning. For these people, the experience was like growing up in a minefield. In addition to knowing explosions were possible, the other crazy making fact was that the position and trigger of the land mines changed from day to day. What got you into trouble today may not set off a mine tomorrow. Clients report having been afraid to walk in the front door of their childhood homes because they never knew what was awaiting them, or a rising sense of fear when they heard a parent drive up because they never knew what mood that parent would be in. Some people grew up without ever having had a consistent environment of trust and appreciation, leaving them anxiously awaiting the next blow-up. For these people, it's not a question of if, but when the good feeling will end.

The following dialogue illustrates this point:

Client: I was always nervous about what would go on, and if the blow-up would be directed my way or not.

Dr. R.: As a child of an alcoholic parent you grew up in a minefield with no safety map. One day you turn right and nothing happens. The next day you turn right again and there's an explosion.

Client: That's exactly how it was. I never knew what would set things off or what would get me in trouble.

Dr. R.: It is very hard to grow up that way. There is never any prolonged peace and quiet. Agitation is the name of the game and one just hopes to get through the day without experiencing too much craziness.

Client: It felt that way most of the time. I never knew how the day would go and now that you remind me of those feelings, yes, I was always agitated and worried when the next shoe would drop. It's like that now, too.

Dr. R.: This is what we have to work on. And one other thing, adult children of alcoholics are not able to feel safe with goodness for too long. They are increasingly agitated because of what you just brought up, always waiting for the other shoe to drop. As goodness increases so does the concern about when that other shoe will fall.

Client: That is just how it feels. I can think of numerous times when I got so nervous just as things seemed to be going well. I almost couldn't stand it, the worrying and being nervous all the time.

Dr. R.: That is a primary cause of self-sabotage. You get in your own way by sabotaging any situation that brings up these feelings. It's almost impossible to remain invested when you are in fear of when something negative is going to happen.

Client: That's true. I know this has happened in my life. Many times.

When children grow up in this climate, they learn not to trust goodness, peace, or success. At any moment, and for unknown reasons, their equanimity might vanish. By adulthood, their unconscious is constantly on the lookout for too much peace, goodness, or success, a conditioned signal for caution or even danger. The concept of being vulnerable (that is, open and available) has become negative, setting the stage for even more difficulties because the prophecy is self-fulfilling. For without openness, it is impossible to have a successful relationship.

Exercise # 1: Changing Your Perspective

Think of a time in your life when you are painfully aware that you held yourself back and did not get what you really wanted. Pick one that is from an earlier time in your life, childhood or your teens, if that is possible. Look at that situation from the perspective of who you are now. Do you see more of what was really going on for you? Are you able to think of other ways you could have handled the situation? What would you do differently if you could go back in time and relive this experience? As you are successful at this, move gradually to time periods closer to the present and try to maintain the same sort of perspective and reflection. This is the perspective you will need to do the work in therapy.

People who grow up constantly on the edge, on guard and without peace, are usually baffled because they consciously believe they "should" be experiencing joy and happiness, but they aren't. Sometimes this gives way to slight depression or melancholia, when a person becomes self critical for not feeling more positive. If anyone criticizes this person's inability to experience pleasure when everyone else is having a good time, the situation can actually worsen as he or she watches for some act of God that might take the good time away.

If your god-like parents took away or sabotaged your sense of goodness, your unconscious sense of how the world relates to you always warns you not to accept good in your life, or at least not to have it for too long, or that other shoe will eventually drop, possibly causing you great pain. To make matters worse, when there is a peaceful or positive moment, you are apt to become anxious. And, rather than to wait for someone else to come along to take away your good time, you may literally end it yourself with behavior that sabotages the experience. In this situation, your unconscious mind wins by lowering the stress caused by the agitation of what you have learned to fear.

The conscious mind on the other hand beats you up for having once again messed up any potential for lasting "sweetness" in life. Hence, you feel like a "loser." Many cry out, "What's wrong with me? Why can't I get it together? I'm an idiot! I should have known better! Why does this keep happening? I can't seem to get a break! Every time I get ahead something sets me back." The truth is that the unconscious sense of survival is stronger than any conscious desire for pleasure, success and abundance, even if that means never embracing goodness or peace. No matter how much you consciously "want" lasting happiness, your unconscious "need" for sabotage will always win. This will continue to happen until your unconscious need is unlearned. To accomplish this, you must do the work.

I often ask my clients if they can describe how a certain behavior or action is serving them. They look bewildered, responding that it does not serve them but rather causes them grief. Yet it must serve them at some unconscious level or it would not be happening. Thus, the unconscious safeguards us even though as adults we may be mystified by our own sabotaging behavior. I respectfully let clients know that this is our work, to bring whatever unconscious reasons may exist to a conscious level.

One client of mine could not understand why he would behave in a way that actually took him further away from his consciously desired goal of getting a date with someone to whom he was attracted. He tagged himself with all sorts of derogatory put-downs and gave me the same dismayed look I so often get from clients when I ask that fateful question: "How does this serve you?" As we explored his worst fears about the matter, he came in touch with how unacceptable he felt in the presence of his would-be date. As a result, the conscious goal of asking her out had been overridden by his unconscious fear of being rejected, a fear that the "little one" within still equates with basic survival or the fear of death.

The Little One

START —7

The little one is synonymous with the inner-child, the part inside us all that feels compelled to hide from hurt in order to stay safe. Each of us has had to survive and attempt to thrive within the less than perfectly healthy systems of our primary caregivers. Only to the extent that our parents were healthy are we likely to be healthy. The rest we have to unlearn before we can learn a healthier, more satisfying way of relating in the world.

The following dialogue illustrates this point.

Client: I am so tired of feeling wrong. It seems that no matter what I do, I never do it quite right.

Dr. R.: Where does this show up in your life?

Client: Everywhere. I can remember as far back as my childhood, my parents never thought much of what I did. They almost never gave me credit for doing anything right, which meant doing things the way they wanted me to do them.

Dr. R.: What do you mean? How would they negate what you did?

Client: Well, they would always take over something I was working on and show me the "right" or "better" way to do it.

Dr. R.: How did that feel to you?

Client: Normal.

Dr. R.: Yes, it was familiar. It was life. It was the way family was for you.

Client: Yes, it was how it was and I didn't know any different.

Dr. R.: That is because it was normal for your family or parent to take over and convey a core message that you were not doing it right and were never going to "get it" so that you could be who and what you want to be. This message gets set in the unconscious place where the self-identity lies and you have a learned family construction that follows you into life later on.

Client: What do you mean?

Dr. R.: It sets up a pattern in which you approach a task with an unconscious sense of failure, and you find yourself not allowing yourself to do all you can to achieve your best.

Client: Is that why I have such difficulty accepting compliments?

Dr. R.: Good insight. Tell me more about that.

Client: Well, I don't really take in compliments from others very well. There are many who really like the work I do, but every time they say so, I just shrug it off. Is this because I feel I can never do it "right enough?"

Dr. R.: Yes. Tell me about the feelings this brings up in you.

Client: I feel sad that this is what I do. I want to enjoy what I do and experience the appreciation of others.

Dr. R.: That is our work, and together we will do the work that needs to be done in this area.

Client: Good, because I am really tired of feeling as though I am not as good as other people.

The twist in our lives comes when we are told on a consistent basis that we are not acceptable. We automatically turn off that part of ourselves our parents or primary caregivers declared as "not good." This begins the process of suppressing the "little one" into an invisible dark area of our psyche. But even more harm is done when we nurture a belief that our "little one" will not get us the love we need. If our parent-gods did not like all of us and loved us more only when we behaved a certain way, then why should we like this "little one" who gets into trouble and is unlovable?

In psychology, this rejection process is called identifying with the aggressor. It may involve cultivating a dislike for a part of yourself that if it had not been suppressed, you might otherwise have appreciated. Remember that children, who are in a survival mode of acceptance and do not process logically, consider only all-or-nothing, black-or-white perspectives. When something doesn't work or they feel criticized, there is no compromise, negotiation, or middle ground. It just is. Therefore, if we are continually told that parts of us are unacceptable, we may discard in ourselves the part that does not seem acceptable, even if this could actually serve us in later life.

I have worked with many adult clients who were terribly ashamed of their own "little one." They had to some extent rejected it. From this learned perspective, they hid this "bad" sense of self away in the caverns of their minds. Thus, the fear of discovery by others keeps that part locked away where no one will see it. Is it any wonder we are not all we can be if our unconscious is dedicated to keeping the "little one" from emerging or connecting with our heart? We can never be complete if part of us is hidden and suppressed by shame. Do you realize how much energy it takes to keep all the "bad" stuff away? People who are using 40% to 60% of their energy to suppress what they are afraid of will have only 60% to 40% available to use consciously in the world. Imagine the amount of energy you would have if 100% of you were available to you!

Exercise # 2: Achieving Greatness

Think of a time in your life when you did something you couldn't possibly imagine yourself doing but you did it anyway and it was a great achievement in your life. What was going on in your life that enabled you to do this? Was there someone or something pushing you and motivating you to go on? Try to think of as many times as possible that this has occurred in your life and try to see the pattern that exists when you are able to achieve the unexpected. As you become conscious of the keys to your achievement, consciously work to bring them into your life on a daily basis. Think of someone you could contact or something you could do that would take you to a new level. Do it now. Do it today.

When the body receives the message to discard feelings, needs, and desires as a protective measure, the psyche does not just lock up the "bad feelings" like fear, anger, frustration, sadness, grief, and pain. It pushes down all feelings. It dampens all emotions, including pleasure, joy, passion, happiness, strength, and power. I help clients work on the causes of their suppressed affect by making it safe for the unconscious to lift its defenses. I often dramatize this by taking my two hands and making a pushing movement from my chest to my abdomen to indicate the suppressing mechanism that occurs as feelings are locked up and stored away. When we stop suppressing the bad or difficult feelings emerge and so too do the positive suppressed feelings. These are the beneficial aspects of the little one that got thrown out with the bath water, so to speak. Often clients ask, "Who will I be when all of this comes out?" My response is, "More. More of everything you can be will be accessed."

The Bible says something to the effect of, "As you see Me so shall I be." In this same vein, Wayne Dyer wrote a book with the catchy, but poignant title You'll See It When You Believe It (1990). The Hindus call life on this plane maya or illusion, and the teachings of metaphysics regard life as the campus for learning our lessons. All these perspectives reveal that our Universe moves in the direction of our belief system. Typically, the internal character scripts we were raised with and have committed to cellular memory are imprinted on our unconscious. Matter has a way of moving in the direction of a self-fulfilling prophesy. That is, it moves in the direction expected of it.

Think of how many times you have been able to complete a previously impossible task and you found yourself saying, "I never would have believed I could do it!" Maybe it took someone to push you beyond yourself or someone who has tremendous faith in you inspired you. In other words, you did it because you couldn't let them down. This person, mentor, coach, or torturer did not complete the task for you, or make you do something you could not actually do. But that individual provided the incentive to get you to go beyond your personal beliefs about yourself. You were able to find more of you than you previously had thought possible.

Until we unlearn it, the learned personality is a roadblock. This unconscious foundation is neither a product of nor is it affected by logic. One does not outgrow it, mature from it, or "get over it." Yet the mighty unconscious can be altered. We can be liberated from its hold on us, with the right tools and the right process.

The following dialogue illustrates that this is possible even after the most difficult childhood.

Client: I'm here because I am well educated but working in a dead end job for ridiculously little money.

Dr. R.: It sounds like you are "under-employing" yourself. This is a situation where your intellect and your ability to do well academically are not in sync with your negative self-esteem.

Client: That's an interesting way of putting it. I do have trouble with not feeling like I can have what other people in my field have. It seems like they know how to do it and I was never given the tools to be able to go after what I want.

Dr. R.: Tell me more about that.

Client: It feels as though all my life I was never given any help to have what the other kids had. They seemed to know what they needed to do and had people to help them and I didn't have a clue what to do or people to help me.

Dr. R.: What was going on with your parents? How did they deal with what was going on in your life?

Client: My father beat us all regularly. He would line us up and have us get prepared while he took us one by one into a room and beat the s—t out of us. We had to listen to the others scream while we stood there waiting.

Dr. R.: That is awful.

Client: He beat us in such an out of control way that I would beg him to stop and offer anything to get him to stop.

Dr. R.: Where was your mother while this was going on?

Client: Often she wasn't home. He would be there while she was working and if he got mad or drank too much he would go off on us.

Dr. R.: Did you ever tell your mother what was going on or was she ever home when he lost it?

Client: I was too afraid to tell her and I believe she knew and just didn't want to confront him.

Dr. R.: Did he ever beat her?

Client: No, for some reason he left her alone. I never knew why.

Dr. R.: What happened when you went to school beaten and alone?

Client: I felt like I do now. Like I had no tools with which to work. I stayed to myself and did not want to get too close to anyone for fear they would hurt me or I might hurt them.

Dr. R.: How did you keep from hurting them or yourself?

Client: I stayed in sports and tried not to think about it.

Dr. R.: How has that worked over the years?

Client: Well, it doesn't work for me anymore. I want a life like other people have. I want to be with someone who loves me and I want to be working at a job that pays me well for my efforts.

Dr. R.: This is a good goal and we will work on the unconscious part here in therapy.

Client: How can I ever have the tools I need if I didn't get them when I was a child?

Dr. R.: The tools you seek come after the seeds of one's self-esteem, worth and confidence have been harvested. Children believe these seeds are the property of their parents. If the parents did not make them grow then how could the child ever make them grow? The truth is that these seeds are __not__ the property of your parents. They are within you. They are your property. Parents, or primary care givers, are the first people who have the ability to water your seeds. If your parents are healthy this happens, but the degree to which they are unhealthy is the degree to which your seeds did not grow during childhood. In your case, your parents had rocks in their watering cans. But as I said, they were the first to have the opportunity to grow your seeds, but they are not the only ones who can do this. We can do this together.

Client: I would like to believe that. It feels like I'm doomed to a lesser life than most.

Dr. R.: I understand that you feel this way. All your life your perceived reality has been that this is it and this is all there is. I want you to know that this reality is a concept learned in childhood. It is something you can unlearn in order to allow your seeds of self-enhancement to grow. This is what I can help you with and we can do here in our work together.

Moving Past Yourself

Generally, people come to psychotherapy when they have a strong sense that their life is not working. Their daily lives reinforce the feeling that they must seek help. Initially they may pray to their maker that whatever process is necessary will not take long and that they will be "cured" quickly. After clients ask about my professional orientation, the next question is usually, "How long will this take?" What do you think your physical trainers' response would be if you were to ask how long would it take to get into shape and stay in shape to be healthy?

Many people who come into therapy are those who have read something about the subject and want to know what more I recommend they read in conjunction with our work. To this I explain that this will not be an intellectual process, though being smart helps. Instead, it is a process of getting in touch with feelings, sometimes very painful ones, plus going back to where the heart first learned how to imagine the self and the way the world relates to the self. Feeding the IQ is not the answer or the way to move forward and it doesn't happen on a specific timetable (this answer does not please a lot of my clients!)

In order to have satisfactory results, one must go beyond the mind and look into the heart and soul where absolute knowing dwells. But most people don't want to hear about this road of the intangible. It is the way, if you will, of faith. There are no quick fixes and the word "workout" takes on a whole new meaning. Yet, in this virtual realm of the unconscious, one can produce substantive and meaningful change. A client may prefer a therapist who caters to the intellect, at least for the time being. Nevertheless, this is merely what the client wants, not necessarily what is needed, and eventually this individual meets roadblocks at the same old stagnant junctures in the road, frustrated and not much further along.

Exercise # 3: Acting On faith

What role does faith play in your life? Faith is when we believe something is true and we act upon it. Were there times in your life when it took faith to get you through? Were there times when you dared to do something incredible based simply on your faith? Write down as many instances as you can of this happening and notice how or where they made your life better. Is there more you could be doing consciously with faith to take your life in a better direction?

I have used the word "faith" for what clients must accomplish as they surrender control to a therapist and trust him or her to move them along the path to change. This comes in time as a relationship of trust builds and the work progresses. The process reminds me of what occurred with settlers who traveled across the plains in wagon trains. Can you imagine one of those pioneers signing on and after walking a while saying, "I don't think I want to go this direction, let's go this way." To arrive at the destination safely, people had to trust that the leader knew the trails along the way. It would have been ridiculous, if not deadly, to take an unknown route just because of a person's ego or desires.

In psychotherapy it is much the same. Once you have agreed to travel across unfamiliar territory in order to reach a land that others have told you does exist, and where you can have a better life, and you have checked out the guide to the best of your ability, you have to let go and pursue the journey. However, you will still need to put in the effort and the time if you want to get something beneficial out of the trip. Just as for the early settlers, you will find that the psychotherapy process takes courage, strength, and determination. And at times the path will be tough. There are no free rides, but endurance is rewarded. The important thing is to show up and be ready to work. It is the therapist's job to guide you along the route you need to take to get where you want to go.

Most people who decide to seek therapy want a different, healthier, better sense of themselves than they currently have. They are no longer content to have their lives running at merely half speed. Those seeking individual psychotherapy are often facing not only a psychological dilemma but a spiritual one as well. They are looking for a therapist who can facilitate their progress past old patterns and who can move them toward a more "quality" sense of their reality. What they tell me for the most part is that they feel an emptiness that leaves them longing for inner peace and emotional fullness, free from sabotage and self-destruction. It doesn't matter whether their problems are in their work or in their relationships. Their bottom line is a desire to have a peaceful and more fulfilling quality of life. And the work we do leads to this goal.

3

Welcoming Substantive Change

✦

The Truth About Therapy

There are those who think psychotherapy is ridiculous. They wonder why anyone would pay someone to be a friend. If psychotherapy were just a "hand-holding" supportive intervention for the friendless, this criticism would be understandable. But the level of work that goes on in substantive psychotherapy is not found anywhere else.

Friends are essential in our daily lives. We hope they are consistent, trustworthy holders of confidence who we can count on to know and care about us. I strongly encourage clients, as they are comfortable with doing so, to seek out and maintain a few close friendships. The reason I say a few is that it takes a great deal of energy and investment to maintain truly intimate, open, close friendships. Those who claim to have many friends are more likely talking about acquaintances. And, these acquaintances are not necessarily there for the deeper, more intimate aspects of relating.

As important as it is to have supportive friends, they are not able to provide dynamic psychotherapy. Many clients report that their friends want to help but cannot relate to their underlying issues. The analogy that illuminates this fact comes from the tree. Friends are helpful in pointing out ways to trim the upper branches. For example, they can detect and eliminate minor issues that block progress. They themselves have all hung out on various parts of the limbs and can thus offer helpful insight. Sometimes this is just what we need in a particular situation. However, when a person is dealing with major life patterns that keep getting in the way of success, the answers are no longer found on the limbs of the tree but in the roots. With deeper issues, friends are probably not able to provide the substantive help that is needed. At these times, a professional psychotherapist is able to navigate the unconscious from which the influences of the learned personality must be ferreted out and unlearned.

The following dialogue addresses this issue.

Client: It feels really bad to have to come in here and pay someone to be my friend and help me figure out what I need to do to move my life along.

Dr. R.: Is this just like what you do with your friends?

Client: No. They get caught up in wanting to solve the problem I'm having. They are truly there for me and I know I can count on them, but the difficulty is they really want me to get over it and move on. I feel like they get tired of hearing my troubles and I don't want to be a burden to them.

Dr. R.: Friends are important for being there when you need them for support and comfort. They are not trained to be able to get to the underlying issues that are blocking you from being able to get out of your own way and create the life you truly want. They want to do what they can, but they don't have the time or the training to help you get at your core issues.

Client: I guess what you're saying is true, but it still feels bad to me to have to rely on someone I pay to help me get on with things.

Dr. R.: If you broke your arm would you go to a physician to set and cast it or would you allow your friends who have your best interest at heart to do the job? Of course you would go to the professional for this. Why do you think it is different when it comes to your emotional well-being and appropriate healing?

Client: I still don't feel right about having to pay someone for the same kind of information that my friends could give me.

Dr. R.: Is the feedback I have given you the same kind that your friends give you?

Client: No, not at all. But it seems like they should be able to tell me the same things and ask the same questions.

Dr. R.: Friends give what they can because they care. Most of what they offer is support or advice that is meant to help you get past the situation or to "get over it." This is why we feel our friends get tired of what we are telling them, because we do not seem to be taking their advice and we're not "getting over it." Then they become frustrated with us.

Client: That is true. After a while, friends start to ignore me. I think they get burnt out hearing the same old story. They seem to think I should just take what they are saying, use the information quickly and get over it.

Dr. R.: That is correct. They are there because they care, but they are not therapists and are not equipped to help you get to the underlying issues that are causing the patterns to keep occurring.

Client: Right.

Dr. R.: Friends are not supposed to have these skills and when they offer all they can offer, they're done. It is in here that you will explore the deeper psychological reasons for your dilemma.

Client: Okay, but that does not mean I'm going to like coming here and paying someone to do this with me.

Dr. R.: No problem. I understand and I will never ask you to like coming here.

Client: Deal.

The early years shape a child's inner reality. Once a person's bottom-line sense of identity and way of experiencing the world is in place, this unconscious, timeless perspective stays with them in perfect working order until it is unlearned. Simply put, psychotherapy is the shortcut to getting out of your own way. It truly allows a person to address core character issues and to experience relief from the pressure of long-term buttons that once pushed lead to panic and acting out.

I often remind clients that even though we do feel our hurt feelings, ironically they won't actually hurt us. Feelings of emotional pain or discomfort, for example, will not hurt you physically or mess up your life; they just hurt. What will really play havoc with your life is trying not to feel, or trying to deny your hurt. This is where people begin to act out their pain with destructive behavior. Inappropriate actions are manifested, for example, by using substances to anesthetize the hurt, getting angry in the wrong places or with the wrong people, or seeking comfort from a person outside of one's primary relationship.

The goal of psychotherapy is to go into the unconscious and to unlearn destructive "reality" beliefs. From this vantage point, one responds from a healthier, broader perspective rather from the narrow ego defenses of childhood. In the microcosm of the child's world, the individual expects to be related to in a certain way and projects this onto the world at large. In the world of the mature adult, this need not be the case. But until the unconscious is unlearned, automatic responses that were imbedded in the child's microcosm continue to dominate choices made in the adult's macrocosm. This is why acting-out occurs and why it subsides in proportion to the unlearning of the unconscious defenses of the microcosm. As this unlearning occurs, you step into a broader world of personal growth and health, a world that offers more security, honesty, options, flexibility, rewards, and joy. Furthermore, this reality is not invested in maintaining a self-image that is unloved, unfulfilled, or unsuccessful.

Even though the goal of allowing yourself to exchange a self-defeating micro world for a more accepting macro one is fairly simple, the process obviously takes some time. When clients ask how long this will take, my response is often unsatisfying for them. But they must understand that the good and the bad news is that we are complex human beings. Undoing learned personality issues does not happen just because we yell at ourselves to "get over it!" To think otherwise perpetuates a superficial, quick fix, fast food mentality that will not work. We must honor the fact that we are, thank goodness, deeper than that.

It Is Frightening

It is important that a person feel some sense of control in therapy. Psychotherapy is a very courageous endeavor. It is much more immediately satisfying to divert one's attention or to anesthetize our feelings through substance abuse. Courage is not the absence of fear or pain, but rather moving on to what you know you must do in spite of these things. It takes courage to confront the demons within and to move with these feelings through the inner labyrinth toward your true path. Therefore, in the beginning, which is usually anxiety producing; it is important to learn to know a therapist as a guide, to feel safe in the process, and to realize that therapy is a choice. This allows people to feel more in control and to be able to tolerate the leap of faith they are taking.

The two most frightening issues people generally bring to their first session are: Will I become too dependent or lose control? And, will I discover something to confirm my worst thoughts about the shadow part of my personality? The more a person is resisting therapy, the more they are likely struggling with one or both of these pre-therapy fears. Those who are not quite ready to engage in therapy are not the people I am referring to here. I am talking about people who want to come, but still protest loudly, becoming adamant that therapy is a joke. It is not easy to come in and face these two issues. One of the most courageous acts is to sit looking in the mirror at the shadow side of your own reflection.

The following dialogue is about these fears.

Client: My biggest fear is that I'm going to find out something awful about myself. I don't know who I'll be when we're finished with our work.

Dr. R.: What is your most awful fear about what you might discover about yourself?

Client: I don't really know, but I have a dread of finding out something about myself that will cause me never to be the same and I will not ever be able to be all right with myself again.

Dr. R.: Every patient I have ever seen initially has this concern. We are sure that the shadow inside of us is a real part of who we are and that this makes us unlovable.

Client: How could it not be who I am or at least a part of me, it sure feels like it is?

Dr. R.: It is a part of the belief system you were raised with and it is such a core sense of your own reality that you have no sense that it is not you.

Client: How could that be?

Dr. R.: How old is your son?

Client: Five.

Dr. R.: Well, if I told your son every day for the next five years that he is an idiot and not worth the time God took to create him, how long do you think it would take before he started believing what I was saying to him? And how long before it becomes more than a belief and actually becomes the core way he thinks about himself and the way the world might look at him?

Client: It probably wouldn't take five years. I see what you mean. It happens so early we believe it's our own idea, and worse yet we believe it's true.

Dr. R.: Great insight. That is exactly what I'm talking about. Now, how long do you think it would take to ease or change that reality? The answer is not as long as you may think. If it is learned and it is not a message from you to yourself, then it can be unlearned when you also take in the feelings you have about the original messenger.

Client: I get it.

Dr. R.: Good, now we're on the same page about what you are not, and working on who sent that message to your self-esteem and messed it up in the first place.

We have all grown up in a society that demands that we manifest a particular toughness, being impervious to attacks or personal vulnerability. This is another reason why psychotherapy seems so frightening. To focus on feelings is often the antithesis of what we are brought up to do. People believe that working with a psychotherapist will be viewed as a weakness or a dependency. This brings about the first fear of entering psychotherapy. The ego tells a person not to turn his or her power over to someone else, which of course sets up a chain reaction of fears and emotions.

I usually ask clients how doing something that enhances self-insight, growth, and personal success can be tagged as a weakness or a crutch. As their guide, I assure them I have no need to help them be anything but self-focused, independent, and personally fulfilled. Working with me, or another qualified therapist, will not create dependence. It is a gutsy quest to become more independent, more of who they truly are. They must rely on my guidance because I know the trails to the place they want to reach. Therefore, they will have to "lean" on me in the unfamiliar terrain they are traveling. I let them know we will move slowly along these trails because, like any skilled guide, I want them to feel and be safe. But after they become acquainted with the terrain and have their own maps, I expect them to ultimately move forward on their own.

The second scariest issue, possibly finding out your personality is as wrong as you were taught to believe it is, relates back to the internalizations from childhood that have been accepted by your unconscious. As a person begins psychotherapy, this learned personality or shadow from the unconscious raises its ugly head and causes a high level of free floating anxiety. In response to this, I usually ask, "What is your most awful fear about what might happen if you do this work?" And, "What are your most dreaded catastrophic fantasies?" We then discuss the demons the person imagines and how these learned internalizations come from how we were raised and not from who we truly are. I add that by uncovering the origins of the demons, they will be able to see themselves clearly beneath all the learned "stuff, excess baggage, shadows, and old scripts." At the onset of therapy it is hard for clients to imagine they are going to find the positive essence of their little one in this way because the majority of us have been brought up to have contempt for this part of ourselves. But instead of discovering a bad seed lurking within, we find there is a curious, sweet inner child to meet and integrate into one's adult self.

The following dialogue demonstrates the way this can work even with the most difficult childhood memories.

Client: (In tears) It is so awful that I was molested and never dealt with it. I remember going to my parents and telling them and all they did was tell me I was lying and that nothing like that could have happened. I was so hurt, but I did what I was told and stuffed it way down inside. I made myself believe that he did not mean it. I didn't want to get anyone in trouble, so I did what I was told.

Dr. R.: What are you remembering?

Client: I remember I went up to my room and cried. I was so humiliated and alone. Then I went to take a shower to wash away the feeling of him and of being dirty.

Dr. R.: Tell me more about feeling dirty.

Client: Well, I can see now that I not only felt that way from the encounter, but I was made to feel that way by the manner in which my parents treated me. I think I must have felt I did something to deserve it.

Dr. R.: Yes. That is the way a lot of people who have been molested feel. They are sure that because it was in some way arousing that they must have wanted it or invited it. But that is not so. The body will respond to being stimulated even when the intellect knows it is completely wrong. But you did not want it nor did you do anything to convey that you wanted this person to overstep your physical boundaries.

Client: I understand what you're saying but it feels so dirty.

Dr. R.: It was a horrendous experience and extremely wrong. Nothing will make it feel okay, nor should it. However, the guilt and blame for this are not on you. What happens when I say this?

Client: I get it, but it will take a while for me to bring it in.

Dr. R.: I understand. It is the first step to not owning this as your fault. What are you feeling as you remember how your parents handled this?

Client: I'm furious. I want to yell at them, "how could you not be there for me, and how could you not believe me and then put this on me?"

Dr. R.: Right. Speak from that place.

Client: I have no words for how angry and hurt I am.

Dr. R.: We will work on that. We will also work more on the issues surrounding the anger and hurt so you do not have to blame your self. This will allow you not to push away those who love you and want to be close to you because you feel unsafe with yourself and the world.

Client: That would be good. I'm tired of keeping those I love at bay, and I'm tired of not getting the closeness I long for.

Another difficulty that makes continuing therapy troubling for some is the possibility that therapy involves some level of blaming your mother and/ or father for how you turned out. Many of my clients don't want to violate or betray the memories of their parents or their relationships with them. While empathizing with their concerns, I tell them that it is not our goal to hate their parents. All humans, including parents, have strengths and limitations and these are inevitably transferred to our children. The Bible states that children will inherit the sins of their father, but I believe we mostly inherit the neuroses of our parents. And this is where environment comes into play in our development.

I tell my clients that I speak fluent family treason. That is, no one is immune to the truth about who must own responsibility for the roots of the family tree, not blame but ownership. Parents set up the system to which children must accommodate themselves; and in this regard, children are victims. Hence, if parents are healthy, the victimization is a good one. The degree to which the parent or primary caregiver is unhealthy is likely the degree to which the child will suffer the wounds of his family neuroses. The work of psychotherapy is not to blame parents but to hold them responsible for the system they created and the impact it had on their children, in terms of self-esteem, self-worth, self-confidence, and self-identity.

The impact the system had on you will reveal why your repetitive patterns continue. As I say to clients, this is not an all or nothing situation. There is good news. There are areas of strength you learned. The good "stuff" is not what is in your way or the reason you seek psychotherapy. Rather, you are at risk due to the internalized wounds you incurred while growing up. So it is not to blame but to see our parents realistically for the flawed humans they are, to understand the impact they have had on us and to move on.

The Place of Knowing

While moving along this practical path, you will ask further questions: Am I still in my own way? Do I repetitively make self-defeating choices? One of the most important concepts in the psychotherapeutic process is the need to differentiate between superficial change and truly substantive change. We know that the road to everything important is through the heart. But this can make us feel vulnerable and open to attack. Clients may want to run the session on a question and answer basis or even be given intellectual reading material in order to make themselves "better." Often, this is their way of accomplishing two things: staying in control and not feeling the anxiety of feeling dependent or weak, and avoiding those dreaded feelings that might make them feel bad or put them in touch with the contemptible shadow of the little one.

Although intelligence and knowledge are helpful tools, our real work is centered in feelings. We need to be more like children, taking in the perspectives and going back to the origins of the unconscious. The heart is where we must go to effectively uncover the microcosmic disturbances of the learned personality.

There is a difference between understanding and knowing. Understanding is the intellectual tap dance of processing strategies about how to proceed in the material or deductive world. Sometimes my clients have already been to other therapists and ask what I will do for them that the others haven't done. To this I pose the following questions. If you understand what is happening or where the problem stems from, why has it not gone away? And, why are you not behaving or feeling in a manner that matches your stated life goals?

Next, I define what I mean by cellular or heartfelt knowing rather than merely intellectual understanding. Most people get this immediately because they haven't been able to effect substantive long-term change with their intellect. I reinforce the fact that they have already done a lot of work and what they understand will indeed help us move along. But the change they are looking for is deeper than the level at which they have been working up to this point.

I continue by asking if there has been a time in the client's life when he or she struggled for a long period to solve a dilemma or question without coming up with an answer. I ask the person to remember the feeling when they finally found one little difference that solved the problem or provided an answer. I ask them to remember that "aha" feeling. Another example of this experience occurs when someone tells you something about yourself but it never quite gets through. Then all of a sudden, the person tells you at just the right time or in just the right way and you have that "aha" acknowledgment of really knowing what they have been trying to say all along. The inner, almost cellular or full body recognition of the "aha" is the place where knowing occurs. It is a physiological "getting it" that cannot be ignored because it rings true through your whole being. Such a moment of insight adds to your repertoire of self; and if you allow it, can produce incredible change.

Once there is an impact-altering experience at the unconscious level, life for the individual must dramatically shift. As one begins to string together various moments of "aha," the pieces of the new reality puzzle slowly assemble so that a whole picture can be completed. Dr. Fred Alan Wolf, in his book The Eagle's Quest, likened this process to the filling in of the grooves of an old record while it is playing, thereby bringing what we are creating to a smooth and level place. And Eric Berne, in Games People Play, explained this idea as a rewriting of old scripts. For me, the important thing is the cellular depth at which true knowing and substantive change occurs. Unfortunately, in America we often seek a short cut around or through something. But the truth is that you may be able to move quickly along your path, but you cannot skip steps.

Individual psychotherapy attends to the center of our internal wheels, from which the spokes of life flow out. This nucleus is where our growth must emote if we are to impact other areas of our lives in a beneficial way. This process is never easy, but it is the essence of getting out of our way. However adept we are, a process is a process is a process. In many cases, the experience and learning we acquire as we are walking through the walls is what allows the outcome to be so worthwhile. We might miss this if we are in too much of a hurry or are focused only on the outcome. When we emerge successfully on the other side of any obstacle, we bring along true knowing to ourselves and to the other people we impact.

<u>Section II:</u>

The Process-Others

✦

Bringing Your Self To
Those You Relate To

4

Bringing Your Self to Committed Relationship Improving Relationships

✦

Choosing Relationships

Whether we are aware of it or not, we choose relationships that help us to learn. Relationships are holy places of learning, cathedrals for the enhancement of the soul. It is here that each of us has our baggage opened up and searched, and our image mirrored back to us in a way only our partner has the capacity to do. What happens in relationships is that we are given the opportunity to confront ourselves with much of what is trapped in our learned personality; we confront ourselves with those parts that need to be exorcised from the self.

To put the words successful and relationship together in the same sentence often seems like an oxymoron, or a contradiction in terms. When I was growing up in West Los Angeles, I hardly knew any kids whose parents were divorced. Today it is rare to meet kids there whose parents are not divorced. And it is even rarer to know an adult who doesn't have an "ex" in their life.

What is going on and how do we change it? What must happen so that our children will not have to go through this experience? What has to happen to avoid having a majority of single parent homes in our country? What can we do so that those who are alone don't remain alone and lonely?

In the movie "Bite the Bullet," with Gene Hackman and Candice Bergman, Candice tells Gene her life story and then asks if he is shocked. Gene turns to her and says, "Lady, the only thing that surprises me anymore is the people some people marry." Sadly, this is the same thing I hear from my clients when they come in for therapy after a divorce. Mostly, they are seeking the answer to the "Y" of the relationship with their "X." Let me be clear, divorce is the worst pain a person can experience in a relationship aside from the actual death of a loved one. Most people don't ever want to suffer this kind of pain a second or a third time. But many, many people would still like to have the joy of a relationship with someone who makes their soul sing.

So what is this thing called coupling that most of our society is doing so ineptly? What is causing our relationships to be non-forever? What is it we think a relationship is? What are we looking for? Mickey Rooney has been married many times. When asked what he thought made a good partner, he said that the first time you marry for love, the second for money, and the third for companionship. Not only do we not know the answers, we don't even understand the questions!

In my opinion, the 1960's ignited the powder keg of tension brought about by the previous decade of so many people feeling lost and undefined in relationships. Thank goodness for people like John Gray (Men Are From Mars, Women Are From Venus) who came along to remind us that men and women are different. And that in order to have successful relationships we need to understand this in our day-to-day interaction with one another. We are still in a period of uncertainty and gender revolution. Often we have no idea how to repair the chaos we have unleashed in our relationships through so many shifts in this area.

Clients who are in successful relationships tell me the key to success is that they are able to get out of their own way because of the insights they get from doing their own work. From a place of wholeness, they feel more able to gain perspective and a sense of humor about their partner's behaviors and responses. Perhaps we should change the marriage vows from "for better or for worse, in sickness and in health, for richer or for poorer," to "as a mirror of life, I will do everything possible to help my partner achieve his or her highest level of being." It is my contention that we need to accept that we are marrying a flawed human being who will make mistakes, and at the same time, become aware of the need to look at one another's mistakes and ask the following questions:

1.   Why does this affect me the way it does? I know in reality this is an opportunity to see in myself the buttons that are being pushed and why.

2.   What is going on in my spouse that would allow him or her to say or do such a thing?

You may think this perspective is not humanly possible. Yet concepts such as these are becoming a major focus of couples that are doing their work and creating healthy, happy relationships. Those committed to becoming better, more conscious partners know that their reactions, whatever the severity, stem solely from their own issues. We know this must be true because we all react differently and to varying degrees to everything that happens in relationships.

If we take it upon ourselves to grow personally, then the whole tenor of the relationship changes and staying together is much more likely. From this perspective of compassion and understanding, we pledge our commitment to the imperfection of each other, rather than to the perfection. We begin with the idea that we are simply at the beginning of who we are going to be. Through the years, each expects the other to become more of what they can potentially be. In this way, we do not enter into a relationship, we do not marry, we do not parent another person, but we literally become a conduit for God and our highest good to allow that person to achieve his or her highest level of being.

The Way to a Better Partnership

The person to whom you are initially attracted in an intimate relationship will have similar values and beliefs, and will have similar desires as you. Most often you will try to find a person who does not have the same land mines as those that blew up your last relationship. After all, you wouldn't let a person like that within a mile of your sanity. Right? But nevertheless, somewhere around the sixth month, at the end of the honeymoon period, you will begin to realize—often to your shock and dismay—that the same patterns of problems are happening all over again.

I often tell my clients that unless they do the unconscious work to unravel their learned personality's sonar, they will just draw to themselves a slightly better version of their past relationships. I imagine it is possible that you could be in an immense stadium with a capacity crowd and still manage to find the one person who is exactly right for you and magically connect with them. If your unconscious is not ready for a healthy relationship however, you will pass right by without even noticing this person exists. On the other hand, if you're in line at the market and the type of person your unconscious needs to sort out old family issues happens by, your sonar will zero in and off you will go on another less than fulfilling relationship ride.

One client of mine experienced this after he left his wife and got involved too soon with another woman. In therapy, I reflected that certain things he was saying about her were leading me to believe he was becoming involved with someone not all that different from the wife he just left. When I told him this, he became indignant and left therapy. Three months later, he called for another appointment. "You SOB," he said. "How the hell did you know she would be just like my ex? How did you know she had exactly the same traits that set me off in my marriage?" In one respect I was sorry I was right. We all deserve to find the "perfect match." But if you do not do your psychological work after a long-term relationship, if you do not learn what you need to know about yourself then you will just be setting yourself up for another opportunity to have basically the same experiences.

At that moment, this man understood. He settled down to do the work of getting into emotional shape. He learned that there are no shortcuts and we cannot skip the required steps. We must all expect that our unconscious is going to take "a pound of flesh" for its growth. If we do not do the work to unlearn our learned personality, then this same part of us will undoubtedly draw unto us the familiar, what to us is "family," like it or not!

Exercise # 1: Understanding Our Reactions

Think of a time when you had a huge argument with your partner. Now, try to step back from that memory. And, from a perspective of compassion and understanding, imagine how you could have both reacted differently. What buttons of yours were being pushed? Was it really about the other person, or was it something within you that caused you to react? What was your role and how could you have created a different outcome?

Just like individual clients, couples are influenced by a society that encourages them to tough it out and to do it themselves. By the time a couple comes into therapy, they fully realize that their life together is not working. They are usually in an emotional state somewhat akin to suicide. They are about to kill the relationship. And, as if this weren't enough, they are often wounded by many years of "doing this" to each other and themselves. Over time, they have become more and more out of sync. The distance they have created allows them to avoid problems and continuously leave their issues unresolved. Sooner or later it is too much, the distance becomes debilitating, even fatal, to the relationship. Because of the emptiness, there is too much room for pain in the relationship. The sad thing is that we have not been taught to think of the health of our relationships in a preventative manner.

Couples almost never engage in pre-marital therapy. They may go to an attorney to make sure their property and wealth are protected, but they won't take the same measures to protect the sanctity of their hearts, and those of their future children. The important point here is that most couples come to therapy just this side of too late. To make matters worse, most husbands are dragged into therapy wondering what good any of this "talking about stuff" will do. Men are not generally inclined to deal with communication or their feelings except with a Mr. Fix-It mentality. As long as things go along according to the status quo and we are left to do our provider thing, most of us men don't recognize that something is amiss until we see that either our wives are not talking to us, or they've stopped having sex with us. Unfortunately, it is usually the absence of the latter that clues us in. All of the sudden we wonder what the heck is going on.

If we men do not get more conscious, we will not have better relationships. This is not male bashing. This is a fact. And, this is not to say that women do not have to shoulder their portion of the responsibility, because they do. When couples expect me to tell them who is to blame, I tell them instead that this is a dance, that they are both partners and therefore share the floor equally. No one likes to hear this of course, but most couples that are serious about change will agree to this fact.

Another difficult point of all of this is that women are usually the first to realize there is a need for counseling. Men are often in denial, well trained by society to suck it up and take it, even if they are unhappy. Although it is usually the woman who wants more in a relationship, men who are in touch with their feelings and desires can also blow the whistle on a partnership. It's rare, but it happens. What is important is not who wants counseling, but the reasons counseling has become imperative.

I focus the couple's attention on the changes that have occurred because certain needs are no longer being met. This helps both people to let go of whatever content (surface) issues may have brought them in, so we can get on with the process (underlying) issues that have been eroding their marriage. I explain that the reason they have come is that one of them has decided the rules of the game (marriage) need to change. It's true, after long years of marriage people change, and what was once a workable way of being together may stop working.

In the initial sessions with a couple I bring myself up to speed on their history and patterns. Many couples are riddled with pain and hopelessness, so I try to give them the sense that I can guide them toward some clarity about what is going on in their lives. We then go further into their wounds and begin a healing process that is long overdue. Needless to say, after many years, sometimes decades of marriage, this is not an overnight process. Emotional wounds need to be addressed carefully and safely. To believe otherwise is wishful thinking. In the first session, it is not appropriate to throw all the "stuff" of the relationship on the table. What really occurs is that the couple "throws up," figuratively, the pain and torment that have accumulated over the years. This pain needs to be disgorged so that these two people have room for new information.

Couples need to have a rationale for therapy that is mapped out so they have a sense of direction and a tangible outline for what is to be done. Of equal importance is that a couple contracts with me to take each step that comes up along the way. It is essential that they are cognizant of the fact that this is work and that it takes commitment and follow through in order to be successful. I also let them know that this is the toughest but most rewarding work they will ever do, no matter what the outcome.

Often one or the other will say, "I don't know if I want to change or undertake this kind of work." I let that person know immediately that this is a choice. It is not for me to force the process, only to guide the journey according to the desired goal. In addition, I do not let either person leave the work without realizing the consequences of their individual choices. I let them know that the issues that brought them into therapy will not disappear and will undoubtedly follow them into the next relationship, should they decide to leave this one, because the unconscious stays with us. It is just like that old saying, "No matter where you go, there you are." Most of the time people realize that what I'm saying is true and they decide to stay in therapy. They just need to know they have a choice; they have the option to leave, and then they feel safer staying.

Content and Process in Couple's Therapy

Of the many aspects of couple's therapy that come into play, perhaps the most important is to know the difference between process and content. Content is most of what the couple has been fighting over—upsets regarding everyday issues. These include conflicts over responsibilities, decision-making, behavior, finances, kids, and relatives. Process issues on the other hand are about emotions, the underlying themes that are at the root of the problems. Process issues are primarily about feelings and the source of those feelings in the learned personality.

For example, a couple may be arguing over the issue of choice. The process issue undermining their focus may be that they are missing each other and not feeling connected, but perhaps there is a battle going on over who initiates outings or trips together. The factors regarding feeling disconnected must be resolved in order for the couple to get back on track. No matter what content issue comes up, it will almost always lead the trained therapist back to an underlying process issue. This is why I tell couples that it really doesn't matter where we begin.

The following dialogues address content and process issues.

Couple Dialogue #1

He says: I don't get it. She comes to me with a problem and all I try to do is help but she ends up yelling at me.

She says: I come to him as my friend and partner to talk about what I'm dealing with and he takes over and tells me what to do, like I'm some kind of an idiot.

Dr. R.: This is not unusual. Men are linear and like to fix things. They are about the bottom line. They want to know the facts, solve the problem, and move on. Women like to feel supported in processing things they are dealing with before they deal with solving the problem. It is important for both partners to let one another know whether they are looking for support or problem solving. If this is not clear from the beginning, women will come to the discussion assuming they will be heard and supported, while men will come to save the day and solve the problem. This lack of clarity sets the stage for conflict. The woman is likely to feel angry that the man is disrespecting her by trying to solve a problem that she is more than capable of solving on her own. And the man feels like he was set up and then unappreciated for trying to help her. The end result is often further disagreement, hurt feelings, and anger.

Couple Dialogue #2

He says: I feel like I'm not appreciated for the things I do. I work very hard for my family and it doesn't seem to be recognized.

She says: I know how hard he works, but he seems to think I get up in the morning, get the kids off to school, and then just hang out the rest of the day.

Dr. R.: Appreciation is one of the missing elements in many marriages or long-term relationships. Men and women have different jobs, even if they both work and take care of the home. It is often the case that couples will get into one-upmanship warfare. This batters both people as they attempt to get the recognition they desire. Often I have to bring people out of the "content" battle and into the "process" issue of appreciation. In many cases each partner is waiting for the other to come forward first before he or she will offer it back. But this will never work.

Couples need to be brought back to a place where they remember they are partners and back each other up without waiting to first be backed up. In this capacity they each provide an invaluable service that allows the other to effectively do his or her job. Without help from one another, nothing will get done at a level that would be considered effective. Once I get them to see this, then they can get back on the same page and begin working together.

Couple Dialogue #3

She says: The most difficult aspect of our relationship is that I'm afraid of him.

He says: What! I have never done anything to harm you in any way.

Couple Dialogue #4

She says: The most difficult aspect of our relationship is that I'm afraid of him.

He says: I wouldn't have to get so angry if you didn't push my buttons in the ways that you do.

Dr. R.: Men need to understand that many women are afraid of our aggression. Even if we do not perpetrate this aggression directly on them, women are intimidated when it is anywhere in their vicinity. It is archetypal, which means that since the days of cavemen women have been uncomfortable when they are too close to male aggression or intensity. It's as though it's in their DNA. Men need to understand this if they are going to effectively communicate with women. It doesn't matter how we men think we are coming across, we need to check in with our women to make sure we have not run them off emotionally or literally.

We men must learn how to get angry appropriately and how to keep our intensity level at a manageable pitch. Because let's face it, we want to be able to get through to our partners and this will never happen if we don't manage the volume control.

Additionally, I want to be very clear: there is no reason for any man to blame a woman for his own anger or for the way he expresses this anger. Of course our partners are going to upset us and push our buttons. As I have stated, it is the nature of relationships that this happens. However, anger or rage that comes out in an inappropriate manner from men directed toward women is the man's responsibility, and no one else's. I have had men in my office literally sit there and blame their wives for the outrageous way they themselves unload on them. But this just isn't right. No one has the ability to cause us to go off half-cocked unless we choose to do so. And if you choose to do it, it is your doing. So just don't do it.

Couple Dialogue # 5

She says: He is so controlling and always talks over me and wants me to agree with his every opinion without ever listening to mine.

He says: She never listens to what I have to say. She turns away or acts as if what I have to say means nothing and that makes me feel bad, like I can never talk to her about what is important to me.

Dr. R.: Men have been brought up to believe in the "men-tality" that what they think or say is right. It is how they have to be in business, providing the right answers without hesitation or ambiguity. They must be self assured and strong in their resolve or they will not be heard or be successful. This leads men to believe they are right and that their opinions are somehow aligned with the pulse of God. As a friend and colleague said to me about his father, "My father believes I have an opinion and he has the truth." Many men believe this is true and continue to bulldoze their wives with their opinions in arguments and debates. This makes women feel steam-rolled and hurt. This attitude paves a path of disrespect and disharmony in a relationship. And, as I always say to couples, "If one of you wins an argument or debate and the other loses, the relationship always loses." Sometimes men will argue, "But this is the way I am and it is what makes me successful in my life." I look at them and ask, "Really, so how's it working in your marriage?" "It's not," they say. "Right," I say.

One difficult aspect of working on core problems is that couples have become steeped in their routine way of arguing. It is not unusual for couples to get caught up in content issues until they get a sense of how to stay focused on process issues. It is not unusual for a good therapist to do a lot of interpreting about what a couple is truly arguing about. Once the couple recognizes the benefit of having a therapist monitor their communication in order to help them stay focused on process issues, they will generally be able to hold off on some of their exchanges at home and wait until they can come in for their appointment.

Exercise # 2: Creating "I" Statements

Write a letter to your partner describing all the things about them that bother or upset you. Tell them about how <u>you</u> feel and what is going on inside of <u>you</u> when things happen with them that upset you. The challenge is to only use the word "you" in the first sentence, the rest is about your own feelings and what is going on inside of you personally. For example, "When you come home late at night from being out with your friends, I feel angry, I feel hurt and afraid because…" and then go on and describe all of the other feelings you have about this. Do your best to describe what is going on inside of you when this happens.

You may wonder how people will ever be able to do this for themselves if they so need a therapist to help them. While there is a certain sense of hopelessness, or at least frustration, that can arise during the beginning stages of the work, I remind couples that they have spent years misreading each other and it is going to take work for that to change. Eventually they will be able to do it for themselves.

Mastering process in a relationship is like learning a new language. Words that used to mean one thing can now have a whole new set of meanings. We wouldn't expect to be fluent in Japanese after just one class, so too we don't unlearn overnight the way we have learned to communicate. Learning a new language doesn't have the pitfalls of emotional baggage and hurtful behavior that most often go along with the negative ways we have learned to communicate in relationships. Learning Japanese might be easier.

Each step of the therapy must be taken very carefully because emotional wounds are easily provoked and years of misunderstandings, usually fueled by false assumptions, must be faced and dealt with. It is important that the couple knows they can rely on the therapist while they are healing and exploring new ways of being together. Rather than being a dependency, this is a courageous path toward a better self, and a better relationship.

Exercise #3: Identifying The Source

Read the letter you wrote in Exercise 2. Try to see the patterns and feelings that show up over and over again in each situation you wrote about. Now, think about when you first felt those feelings. Was it in your youth or your childhood? What is the source of the feelings? What sets you off when the button is pushed? Often, just knowing where the feelings originated is enough to diffuse emotions that arise in you.

5

Bringing Your Self To Parenting

✦

Understanding Adolescents

This chapter deals with parenting, another step in the journey of life. The simple fact is that the more work you do, the fewer family generational neuroses you will pass on to your children. Because infants and small children are not my primary expertise, I focus in this chapter on an area that is near and dear to my heart: adolescents. For many people, this is a frightening topic. Parents are usually not at all clear about how to handle this stage of their children's lives. Even therapists make the mistake of thinking they can treat teens in the same way they treat adults. Such therapists may experience themselves on the defensive, get into trouble soon thereafter, or more typically, find that the adolescent drops out of therapy because of lack of rapport.

Several aspects of the psychological phenomenon of teenagers must be understood before a therapist can successfully approach a teen client. The first thing to know is that there are three distinct stages of adolescence. The first stage of adolescence is marked by an urge to separate and individuate from the family in an effort to develop one's own ego or sense of self. In the beginning of this process, teens focus their ego or sense of self on the next best "family," which is their peer group. They become preoccupied with the "norm" as defined by their peers. They move away from what parents and society say is the norm and link up in dress, language, and music with their own peer group. Teens are less interested in school for the education offered and more because it is the place where they see their friends. They are predisposed to testing how far they can bend rules they didn't have any say in creating. They are constantly checking out how their image measures up to others, and they are plagued by constantly changing hormones. With their physiology out of control, adolescents are at the whim of new emotions that they haven't a clue how to interpret or manage.

Middle stage adolescents are preoccupied with proving they are no longer children in any respect and can be a force to be reckoned with. They are on the move, and convinced that they are more than ready to handle their own lives. During this stage, I often remind parents that, as much as is possible, teens need to be given more slack within appropriate limits. In just a few years, when they are eighteen, they will be on their own. The goal is to prepare them to handle work or college in an adult fashion. Middle stage adolescents are thinking more adult thoughts as well as having more adult feelings about the opposite sex. The middle stage is the trial and error forerunner to adulthood. And as with any new learning, there are bound to be mistakes. Parents need to focus on being vigilant guides during this time, rather than staunch leaders.

These teens look and act most like the picture of adolescents adults recognize and fear. They are for the most part fully grown, fully developed, and full of themselves. All of this is appropriate, though at times difficult to deal with. Teens are not, as most parents assume, out to get us. They simply need to explore this new realm called non-childhood. The trick is to let the teenager explore while still maintaining some level of sanity, theirs and yours. Parents need to be able to step back and loosen the reins in direct proportion to the amount of responsibility the adolescent can manage.

The late stage of adolescence is typically the end of teen hell. Some adolescents, who were not allowed to make enough of their own decisions, are frightened of moving on. Those who were held onto too tightly will show increasing rebelliousness during this stage. But for most families, this is the time when the craziness abates. Your teen will see their peers taking college entrance exams and thinking about life after high school. During this stage most teens realize that adulthood is around the corner and that it is time to get serious. They are thinking about what job they will get or which college they will attend. Gradually the chaos created by the need for separation begins to ebb.

Generally, after teens are out of the house, either away at college or working, they begin to reconsider their parents and come to see them as reasonable people. Mark Twain said that early teens are appalled by what their parents do not know and, by the time they become young adults, shocked at how much their parents have learned. As the cellular need to rebel and find one's self mitigates, parents are seen in a better, more realistic light. And so, later stage teens stand on a more comfortable platform from which to relate to their families; and families can breathe a sigh of relief and begin to heal.

The most important fact to remember about adolescents is that they change every two years. There is no other time in life that human beings predictably go through complete restructuring over a six-year period. Adolescents are transforming physically, intellectually, chemically, cognitively, socially, psychologically, spiritually, and philosophically. And they are typically no longer anchored by the stability of family because of their need to identity with their peers. Considering all of this, when you think you are going through a lot with your teen, just try to imagine what they are experiencing in comparison.

As adults seek out others they can choose from a wide variety of ages and people. We think nothing of having a friend who may be two, five, or ten years older or younger than we are. We also choose people from various groups. For the adolescent, someone two or three years different in age is considered either a child or an adult. A thirteen year old would find it insulting to hang out with a ten year old. And, although a thirteen year old might think it an honor to be invited along with a sixteen year old, the peer pressure would be extreme.

Teens consider others who are three years younger or older to be in a completely different world than they are in. You'll see this if you watch any of the movies from my list of recommended films depicting adolescent group identification. Teenagers have an adversity to hanging out with anyone who is even remotely different from them. They make very little room for someone who does not wear the same clothes, listen to the same music, or see life in the same way. This may be because teens encounter new situations so often in their lives that they need people of like mind to act as anchors for them. They cannot always trust their experiences and they need others who will mirror these back for them in a way that is consistent with their own thoughts and feelings.

How many of us would choose to go out everyday and be forced to function this way? My guess is that most of us would suffer from extreme frustration and depression if we had to face this in our daily lives. The mere thought of dealing with life at such an intense level would terrify and exhaust us. And yet, we yell at our teens for not "using their heads." Why is it that adults have forgotten how hard it is to be an adolescent? Generally speaking, teenagers are accurate when they accuse us of not understanding.

This is Normal

Adolescents are genetically predisposed to create distance from their greatest source of support, their parents. It is part of their psychodynamic makeup to work at not identifying with, or to some degree not relating to, their own families. When was the last time your teenager willingly went along on a family outing? When was the last time your early adolescent kissed you in front of friends? Teens are appropriately engaged in separation and individuation, primarily from their families. It is a time for them to identify with peers and to seek out their place in the pecking order.

Again, the most important thing for parents to remember is that teenagers are transforming all aspects of their being every two to three years, so it's no wonder they may be having a hard time. Maybe you, as parents, could approach their craziness and acting out with more compassion, realizing that this chaotic passage is part of growing up. Not that troublesome behavior should be overlooked but it can be handled compassionately. I often tell parents that the reason teens feel adults do not understand them is mostly because they do not understand themselves. Discussing and supporting the process (the why) of their problems, which is the underlying reason for what is occurring will help them progress more quickly and effectively.

The ego of a teen is placed differently than that of a child or an adult. An infant expresses its ego through the mouth; the child through the family; and an adult through work and family. For the teen, ego is identified through their peer group. A great old movie that depicts peer identification in the extreme is *The Wanderers*, in which the characters are completely wrapped up in the clothes they wear, the music they listen to, and the camaraderie of their "pals." This movie also accurately depicts body image as a major preoccupation of teens.

At preadolescence, about age eleven or twelve (what the media is calling the "teens"), parents feel their children distancing and pulling away from them. Unfortunately most parents respond at this point with techniques that worked when their sons or daughters were younger. That is, they become controlling and/or punishing. There are very few sources that tell parents that what has worked up until now will, for the most part, not be effective from here forward. This leaves parents feeling out of control and frustrated. It has taken them years to develop the skills to get this far and now it feels overwhelming to try to integrate new skills. Parents are interacting with a whole new level of person in the adolescent.

Adolescence truly is the path out of childhood and into adulthood. Not only are teenagers walking a trial and error line between two paradigms, so must parents if they hope to succeed in helping their adolescent children become functioning adults with appropriate boundaries and adequate balance in their lives.

An example I often give comes from my work in the Adolescent Medicine Division at Children's Hospital in Los Angeles. Some years ago I covered the unit that handles teens undergoing medical procedures. I remember being with a sixteen year-old boy when a resident came in to talk about a surgery the boy was scheduled to have the next day. While the resident anxiously explained the surgical procedure, the teenager tried to be the brave adult he expected himself to be. After the resident finished her explanation, she asked if the boy had any questions. The teenager said no and so the resident left the room. After she left I asked the boy whether he really understood what was about to happen and how he felt about it. Immediately, he broke into tears and told me that he didn't understand and that he was scared. This example illustrates the degree to which we must be sensitive to the two sides involved in working with adolescents: the child and the emerging adult. The resident had attended to the adult side of this patient but had overlooked the feelings of the child. Only half of the individual had been considered.

Working with adolescents is complex and involves more components than working with patients in other age groups. A reverse example is about a sixteen and a half year-old boy I was working with in my practice. He was furious with his father for not considering that he was capable of thinking for himself and had independent opinions and feelings, different from those of his father. One time while he was shaving before school, his father had come into the bathroom. The father was somewhat startled to see that his son was already shaving. This surprise angered the boy because it reflected denial on the part of the father who had been tending only to the child side of the son and not acknowledging the emerging adult.

The balancing act of raising your teen is at the crux of the matter. This is complicated by the fact that amid all of this trial and error the teen still relies heavily on the parents for guidance and to set limits. This bewilders most parents who wonder how this can ever be successfully accomplished. One of the first things I do is to supply these parents with my lecture tape, "Surviving Adolescents," which is about defining, understanding, dealing with and parenting a teenager. After listening to this they most often come back more receptive and ready to embrace this new stage of parenting.

I also encourage parents not to take the changes in their teen personally. Parents may get angry with their son or daughter for pushing them away or for not being as close as they once were. They act as if their child is consciously and maliciously doing something to hurt them. Unfortunately, parents can often be controlling and at times even vindictive because of these feelings. By getting upset, they are telling their teens that it is wrong to be doing what is natural and appropriate for them to be doing. This only produces a tug of war in which no one wins. It also instills guilt in adolescents who may then also become frustrated and angry. Many parents really lose sight of the prime objective in raising children: to bring up individuals who are healthy, functioning adults, able to leave the nest. Even though many parents might never truly be ready to let go, especially in the early stages of separation and individuation, they need to facilitate this process, allowing for it in moderation.

A further part of the letting go process for parents is grieving the increasing loss of contact with a child who is becoming an adult. Parents can have empathy, compassion, and support for one another because they are going through this together. Of course, some parents say to themselves, "Not me, I want my child to grow up and it doesn't bother me in the slightest that he doesn't want to spend as much time with me. There is absolutely nothing to grieve." But it is normal for parents to feel sad when a child won't kiss you in front of friends, or stops coming over to nestle their head on your chest, or seems not to need your protection.

It is natural to feel a loss as you experience a shift in the way your child relates to you. It is as acceptable for parents to grieve as it is for teenagers to change. Furthermore, you can grieve and still be okay with their growth and separation. When you are conscious of your grieving, you'll be less likely to react by trying to over control your teenager's life, which will only cause conflict and the family as a whole to lose.

The next important lesson for parents to learn is that unlike when a child is younger, with an adolescent everything becomes a negotiation. It is no longer the case that when you tell your teens to do something they will simply do it. When I was working at Children's Hospital, I received a call from a mother who was hysterical. She was sure her son had gone crazy. I asked what made her think this and she said that until recently he had been a very good boy who was polite, did his homework, talked to her about his day, and was very responsible. But lately, he had turned into a "Mr. Hyde." He no longer acted responsible, was cutting classes, was not talking to her, liked staying in his room, and talked back to her for the first time. I asked how old he was and she said thirteen. I told her there was nothing to worry about but that she could bring him into the clinic if she felt it was necessary. Before I hung up the phone I said, "Mrs. Bradley, welcome to adolescence." I probably shouldn't be so glib, but it always makes me chuckle when parents forget their own teenage years and are caught completely off guard by the changes in their teens.

For the most part the days of telling your teen what to do are over. There are some times when it will still be appropriate but you must choose these times wisely and with discretion. Save the "because I am your parent" rap for serious battles. Of course you will need to intervene if your teenager is heading into clear and imminent danger as in drugs, illicit sex, or crime. But otherwise negotiation seems the only platform from which to guide a teenager. Even if it was natural for parents to govern from a place of control when their child was younger it behooves them to find a new way now. The genetics of a teenager are geared to fight and to separate. They will rebel even more, and in much less healthy ways if they feel they have no say in the decision making process as it relates to them.

What we want to give our teenagers are the tools with which to handle adulthood. Do we want them to bow down to authority? Do we want them to cave in every time the situation gets tough? Do we want them to think they are free to do what they want without paying their dues? Or, do we want them to understand the consequences of their actions? If we expect them to jump to our tune without thought, if we expect them to obey without question, if we teach them that limits are just for the suckers who can't manipulate the system, and that agreements are things imposed on them, what kind of adults will we be raising?

As I have said, I speak fluent family treason. You will not hear me support the line I often hear from adults that "Children have to respect their parents!" Who says so? In my talks and in therapy, I often say that the eleventh commandment was left out of the bible. It would have read, Honor Thy Children. Respect and honor are earned not deserved. Anger and violence support aggression and rage. The best way to bring up a healthy adolescent, who acts in intelligent, original, and creative ways, is to listen! Listening is the way to begin any negotiation.

One of the ways I suggest that parents get in touch with the world of teens is by watching the movies *The Breakfast Club* and *Sixteen Candles*. These two films give parents an accurate glimpse of the ways in which teenagers focus their identification and priorities.

Effective Negotiating

The first step in negotiating with your adolescent is to view him or her as a person rather than as a child. You may tell me that you are already doing this and it isn't working. But my experience is that most parents would never dream of working out something with their friends in the same manner they do with their teenagers. How many of you have walked into your teenager's room and told him to take out the trash or to do the dishes "now!" If you had a friend over who was going to help out with chores around the house, and if that person were watching TV or talking to someone on the phone, would you demand that she stop what she is doing immediately and go do the chore? Of course not! Why not? Because it would be very disrespectful. And yet, how many of you have done this same thing to your teenager?

If you truly view your teen as a person of worth, why would you do this? Do you have so little respect for your teen that you think he should just put down whatever he is involved in at the moment and do what you say? If you understand what the peer group means to an adolescent how can you not understand how important talking on the telephone might be to your teen? You feel entitled to interrupt because you see them as your kid. This approach may have worked when they were under the age of eleven, but it will destroy family harmony to do this with a teenager.

What would you do if you came to work late and your boss, who was having a tough day, decided to dock you a whole day's pay for coming in late? Most of you would be outraged. You wouldn't stand for it. You would demand to know how such unfair punishment could be levied against you for such a small infraction, especially when no one had ever warned you this would be the consequence. Would this have the affect of making you feel more or less respectful toward your supervisor? Would this make you feel closer to your supervisor? Would it make you want to spend more time with him? My guess would be "not." And why would your teenager feel differently when you inflict extreme measures on him? Why would they choose to relate to you when you impose limits where previously there were no rules? If you as an adult would not stand for that kind of treatment or would never consider imposing such a thing on a friend or colleague, how can you do it to your adolescent and say you treat him or her like a "real person?" How can you believe you are preparing your child for the "real world" by doing these things?

Once you begin to see your adolescent as an individual you can begin to negotiate in good faith. Teens will respond because the child side of them knows there must be limits and the emerging adult needs the respect they feel when given options. I know it is difficult to even imagine that teenagers actually want limits, but children of all ages beg for them. They will push the envelope to the maximum, trying your patience until you give them boundaries. Sure, they will say they love freedom and don't want rules. However, children intrinsically feel loved and protected when parents set rules and consistently enforce them. Teenagers know that parents are the ones they have to deal with when expanding their options. Nevertheless, they need to have their emerging adult tended to as well. Adolescents will negotiate in good faith. The faith is broken only when they feel you will not meet them half-way. This is when they will begin to take matters into their own hands.

Some of you might be saying, "Well, this is just great. If we don't cater to the needs of this emerging adult then we can expect anarchy." In some respects this is true. And wouldn't you expect the same from anyone else if you were trying to keep them down or take away their freedom? If someone attempted to limit your personal rights, wouldn't you fight? Isn't this how wars are justified? Adolescents are struggling for their rights. If you deal with them from a place of respect and fairness, they are much more likely to deal with you in the same way. Teens neither want to leave their families nor stage a mutiny. At some level, they know they have it good. They only entertain these thoughts when it seems to them that their ability to "grow up" is being sabotaged.

So, in what ways can negotiating come from a place of respect and good intent, and how does one apply this effectively with a teenager? Two principles serve in raising healthy adolescents. First, there are only a few areas not open for negotiation. These are school, substance abuse, and criminal behavior. And second, well-equipped adults emerge when teens are allowed to show what they cannot do. This means letting them demonstrate their limitations while enforcing necessary boundaries and consequences. This helps parents remove themselves from the authoritarian enforcer position and focus on being positive role models and guides.

Let's start with principle number one. There should be no discussion about whether a child will go to school or do their schoolwork. An appropriate grade point level is the job of the adolescent. There are no exceptions. But negotiations can determine what will happen in terms of rewards or punishment if the teen does or does not accomplish this goal. This is an important issue that most families face, so let's take some time and move slowly. First, children need to understand the goal, passing their classes. Furthermore, it must be made clear what passing means. There are many teens who think a D is a passing grade. I tell parents that anything less than a C is considered unacceptable and warrants a consequence.

Each family has the right to negotiate the bottom line, the specific goals. In addition, students can be encouraged to do A and B work through a system of rewards, along with information about the connection between good grades and better colleges. But grades are not the only issue. The key to any effective negotiation is deciding what action to take. Research shows that if all members of the process have a say in the discussion, everyone involved is more likely to accept decisions and carry them out.

Decide together with your teenager what the reasonable consequences will be. For instance, if the teenager says she feels the result of a D grade should be no phone calls, this is obviously too light a consequence for a serious lack of study and discipline. However, if the parents say being grounded until the next report card should be the consequence, this is too severe. The appropriate action is most likely somewhere in the middle of these two extremes, but negotiation and agreement from both parties are keys to success.

I believe in finding a punishment to fit the crime. If children steal money from their parents, not letting them go out with friends for a month does nothing to correct the crime or teach the value of money. You would not expect your boss to take away your best client as a way of teaching you a lesson about not being late for work. There is no correlation. This kind of punishment only causes low morale and feelings of anger. As your teen makes mistakes, it is your job to reveal the errors of their ways in a manner that allows them to do better and to regain your trust.

A typical issue with teens is that parents find out, usually too late, that the adolescent has not been turning in homework. Many parents want to lower the boom and incarcerate their teen for the rest of the semester. I understand this reaction and I strongly suggest not doing it. Such punishment does not fit the crime and will not lead to the desired results of discipline, responsibility, and follow through. I understand a parent's initial reaction to punish but I suggest stepping back and counting to ten. Once you overreact it is hard to take it back and this damages the way you are seen by your child. There is always time to react. Allow yourself time to regroup, perhaps talk to your partner or spouse, and decide on a strategy. It is very important that teenagers see their parents and caregivers as united. Your child knows consequences are coming, so letting him worry about it a little is not a bad piece of strategy. This allows you to gather your senses and make decisions that will serve the best interests of everyone involved.

One effective way of handling the issue of missing homework is to let your child know how disappointed you are and that it is clear to you that he is not able to handle this on his own. Remember, adolescents do not like to think of themselves as not being able to handle things or as too young or immature in any way. When you say you are disappointed in them it really hits home. It implies that they have taken a step back in their level of maturity and they really hate to hear this. You can then set up a weekly accountability sheet to see if all their assignments have been turned in. If assignments have not been turned in or if the sheet is not signed by every teacher, then the agreed upon consequence will be enforced. By doing this, you are teaching your son or daughter to be responsible for homework as well as for the sheet of paper. The consequence is carried out for missing assignments, or for not handling the responsibility of getting the sheet signed.

The consequence of not carrying out this job is part of the ongoing negotiation and needs to be fairly strict. For example, the adolescent is not allowed to go out on the weekend following any failure to turn in homework or have the homework sheet signed. Some parents may feel this consequence is too light but this is not about imprisonment, this is about learning lessons. Consequences are important, and so too are built-in vehicles to regain trust and privileges. If teenagers do not see a light at the end of the tunnel, they will not be motivated to improve. Remember, a teenager's ego and their life links are attached to their peers. When not allowed out with their friends, teens miss out. If you feel this is too easy, you can throw in no phone calls. But the teen must have some say in this. She may come back with the idea of restricted calls instead of no calls. I invite you to think about compromise, knowing that adolescents are more apt to go along with the program if they have some say in it. The good news is that instead of fighting over the consequences, they will comply and this will make your home a much more peaceful place. The gist here is to understand how negotiations can work and that through these parents are still setting limits and guiding their children but in a much more peaceful way.

The second principle is about being effective with your adolescent without becoming the heavy. Teenagers need as much rope as necessary to hang onto or to hang themselves. It seems to me that parents get too caught up in letting their teens know where they expect them to mess up. I've had a number of teens come into my office saying, "If my parents keep expecting me to do this bad thing, I might as well do it and get it over with." Parents who focus on what they believe teens can do well and right raise positive people. As adolescents struggle to deal with their constantly changing world, they are worried enough about not measuring up or doing things right. They do not need parents at home giving them the same negative messages they fight off all day at school. I advocate allowing them to make the attempt to handle it and to grow in the process, and to see how it goes. If it goes well, reward them with praise, respect, and further privileges. If it goes badly, deal with the situation through the limits you have already outlined with them.

An excellent example that I believe illustrates this concept applies to the desire of an adolescent to extend the bedtime hour. Many parents have experienced this. Often a control battle ensues around whether or not the teenager is able to stay up later and still get up and ready for school the next day. The argument is an academic one because there is no proof at the time to verify what the adolescent can or cannot handle. The whole issue boils down to whether or not the teenager is able to convince the parent to give it a try. Typically, parents go into control mode, mentally trying to figure out if the adolescent has in some way "earned the right" to stay up later. This puts parents and their teens at odds in a conflict that diminishes family stability.

Parents end up being the heavies with teens "working" them in order to get what they want.

And what do they want? It seems that teens who are asking for more privileges are saying they feel more grown up and can handle a new situation. And isn't this what we want them to reach for and to learn to do? This is a skill we want them to have for adulthood. We should be thrilled when teens get a good gut sense of what they can and cannot effectively handle. So why do parents get caught up in squelching these early teen forays into assessing their instincts? Why not let them see for themselves (and for us) what they can deal with? Why not get out of their way and let them try?

Say to your teen that you want him to do more and are willing to give him as much freedom and as many options as he can responsibly handle. In this case, let him know that if he goes to bed at a later time and is able to get up the next morning without being moody or grumpy, get to school on time, and come home without an attitude based on fatigue, then you will renegotiate his bedtime. And if the next day he accomplishes this feat, then I suggest you reinforce his appropriate estimation of what he is able to do. He was right about what he can handle. Of course, in order to keep the new bedtime, responsible behavior must continue.

On the other hand if your teen is unable to get up or shows blatant signs of fatigue, then you do not have to hassle her, yell at her, get controlling, or have a fight. All you have to say in a normal tone is that she is not quite ready to take on this new hour and can try again some other time. In this manner, you are not obliged to play the enforcer or the antagonist. And, you have facilitated a real testing ground in which you can support your adolescent's effort to succeed. This is a great place for you as a parent to align with your child's attempts to grow up, by guiding rather than fighting. By going with your teen's energy to expand his or her world, you can also enjoy the process and not have to feel awkward or in the way.

Parents who reward adolescents and rejoice in their efforts ensure their children's success more than anything else. And when teens do not succeed, parents can be empathetic to their disappointment without being blamed. Let teens show what they can or cannot accomplish. Don't be their scapegoats. It is so much more fun to be on the cheering side of parenting than it is to be on the side of the inquisition.

This attitude applies to any new thing your teenager wishes to attempt including sports, parties, curfews, hobbies, dating, and so forth. Success is based on whether or not the new experience is handled responsibly, making sure nothing gets in the way of an adolescent's main job, which is school. It is very important for adolescents to have the full extent of the freedoms and options they can responsibly handle. Isn't this how real life works for adults? And isn't real life what we are preparing them for?

Recently, I met with a young man who was having problems getting along with people, especially his parents. It was his parent's idea for him to come to counseling. But toward the end of our first meeting, before his parents joined us, he and I had this short conversation.

Dr. R.: How are your sleeping and eating patterns lately?

(He assures me that though appropriately upset he is not at risk or a candidate for medication.)

Dr. R.: Is there any more you want to tell me at this time?

Client: No.

Dr. R.: Okay. How do you feel about seeing me for some sessions and seeing if I can help with what is going on?

Client: Okay.

Dr. R.: I'm going to bring your parents in and we'll talk with them and set things up.

Client: Okay. I didn't think I would come back.

Dr. R.: What changed your mind?

Client: I feel a little better about things.

(Then his parents come into the room and the four of us are together.)

Parent: He has A.D.D.. Between the anger, the arrogance, the lack of discipline and the lack of focus he is really trying our patience.

Dr. R.: Has anyone suggested that you read <u>Driven To Distraction</u> by Edward M. Hallowell, or talked to you about the way most boys act when they have A.D.D. or A.D.H.D.?

Parent: No one told us about that book, but we have talked to his teachers and read about it on the web.

Dr. R.: I strongly recommend that you read <u>Driven To Distraction</u> and I have a cassette tape I did on boys with A.D.D. that will help you get a sense of what you already experience but may not understand. So many parents think their sons are lazy and just need to try harder. It is more profound than that and there is more physiological information that you need to be aware of.

Parent: Well we might need to understand more, but he has got to deal with school and home better. He is driving us crazy.

Dr. R.: I understand. He is lacking in discipline, focus, and the ability to concentrate. He is arrogant, argumentative, controlling, needs to be right, and needs to have the last word.

Parent: That's it.

Dr. R.: Is there anything else I need to know about your concerns or things at home before I meet alone with your son?

Parent: He has been lying and we can't trust him.

Dr. R.: Okay. Now if you will excuse us I will talk with your son. And, unless there are any concerns for safety or abuse issues, what he and I talk about will remain confidential.

(And then the parents leave.)

Dr. R.: So what did you think about what they had to say?

Client: I don't know.

Dr. R.: Well, how did you feel about what I had to say about guys who have A.D.D.?

Client: I've heard it before.

Dr. R.: What do you think about what you have heard?

Client: I don't care.

Dr. R.: Let me tell you, I have worked with a lot of boys who have A.D.D. and every one of them has an above average intelligence and are pissed off that they cannot compete on school exams. What do you think about that?

Client: I know. It sucks. No matter how hard I study, even with a tutor, I never do well on any of my tests. People know I have A.D.D. because of the special ed. courses I'm in and they call me stupid.

Dr. R.: I know. The other guys I work with feel the same way. They feel stupid and inferior and like "what's the use."

Client: Yeah, what is the use?

Dr. R.: Well I'll tell you. First off, has anyone ever told you that A.D.D. starts to lighten up after the age of eighteen?

Client: No.

Dr. R.: I can't tell you why this happens, but it does. In college, studying and discipline are easier. Not easy, but easier. But you have to hang in through high school and get at least Cs. This is your job and all the freedom you want hinges on this. I will help you to achieve more if you set your goals on Cs and I will help your parents to understand this. What do you think?

Client: Even C's are hard for me.

Dr. R.: I know, but with effort and tutors you can pull it off.

Client: If they would back off of me and not push so hard, I could probably do that. But they are too strict and they won't let me go out with my friends,

Dr. R.: I will explain more at another time about A.D.D. and what you need to be aware of. But you have to hear that rewards and consequences are part of the deal. Okay?

Client: Okay.

Dr. R.: Now what is the deal with lying?

Client: I get into so many fights with my mother that they never want to hear what I have to say. I also want them to just let me do the things my friends do.

Dr. R.: Lying is typically an adolescent's way of saying that no matter what they say they will not be believed, so they might as well lie. It is also a situation in which you feel nothing you say or want is going to be listened to or agreed to so why not lie as a way of getting what you want.

Client: *How did you know that? My parents don't seem to believe me when I tell them the truth and they won't let me do what my friends are doing.*

Dr. R.: *Okay, I get it. You can earn your freedom and time with friends, but you are going to have to earn them through your behavior, including finishing your homework and getting better grades. First, I'll talk with your parents about not entering into war with you, but you have got to back off of being so angry and having to have the last word. I know this is hard because all the A.D.D. boys I have worked with have the same problem, but if they back off some will you?*

Client: *I'll try.*

Dr. R.: *I'll help you with this and give you other ways of communicating, but you are going to have to do more than just try. You will have to do it, and I know it will be tough for you.*

Client: *It will be.*

Dr. R.: *Are you willing to work with me toward this?*

Client: *Yes.*

Dr. R.: *Okay, I'm going to invite your parents in to talk more about this. (Parents come back into the room.)*

Dr. R.: *Your son has agreed to continue with sessions. He has heard from me that he is going to have to learn some new skills and there are things I need from you as well. Okay?*

Parent: *We're pleased he'll get some help and we're willing to do our part.*

Dr. R.: *Good. First, you must read Driven To Distraction. It will help you understand how not being able to compete at school while being so bright is like a curse that causes huge inferiority for your son. Second, in every family with a son who has A.D.D. there is one parent who gets into more control battles than the other. It is not due to gender and typically the other parent has a better time getting along. In this case it is the mother who is over controlling. For a while, I would like it if dad could do as much of the interacting as possible. Third, over the course of a few weeks we will talk about a strong behavioral program, which we'll put in writing, pertaining to school and home. And fourth, I want you to listen to my tape on A.D.D. as it will give you a lot of information and answer questions you may have. Okay?*

Parent: *Yes, we want things to be better.*

Dr. R.: *Better is possible, but it is going to take some time. Nothing about this is easy and it will take everyone doing things differently.*

In another session, I had this conversation with two parents and their adolescent daughter.

Parent: *She thinks she is old enough to do her own thing. It's as if we don't matter or aren't the parents anymore.*

Dr. R.: When did this start?

Parent: It started when she got into high school and we tried to give her more freedom. It is also because her friends changed and we are not so pleased with who she is hanging out with.

Dr. R.: If your daughter's friends are into drugs or crime then you must step in. What are you most concerned about when it comes to these new friends?

Parent: They dress like gang members in those baggy pants and always in black. I also don't think they are doing well in school.

Dr. R.: Okay. What is your biggest concern about your daughter?

Parent: We're worried that she is getting on the wrong track and we want to nip it in the bud before there are serious things to worry about.

Dr. R.: What is your worst fear about the future?

Parent: We're concerned about drugs and her not completing high school and having a successful life.

Dr. R.: Okay. Now if you would wait in the outside room while your daughter and I have a talk. And, outside of any concern about safety or abuse, the conversation she and I have will remain confidential.

(The parents leave the room.)

Dr. R.: So, what did you think about what your parents had to say?

Client: They worry about everything. I am not even half as bad as they say.

Dr. R.: Why are they so worried about you? Are you messing up in school and are your friends people your parents should be worried about?

Client: No way. I just don't want to let my parents in on everything I'm doing. My grades are As and some Bs, and my friends are for the most part doing well in school.

Dr. R.: For the most part?

Client: Well some of them are not into school and do smoke pot.

Dr. R.: And what about their clothes? Are any of them into crime or gangs?

Client: That is so bogus. I cannot believe they think that. My friends dress just like most teens out there. My parents are so straight that they have no clue what is cool and what is criminal.

Dr. R.: Well put. So what do you think we need to do here?

Client: I think my parents ought to get real and not be so strict.

Dr. R.: So let me see. Everything they said was out to lunch and not a word of it has any merit?

Client: Look, they mean well and they're good people, but they have forgotten what being a teenager is all about. All they see is the negative and they expect the worst. I am sick and tired of being told that my life is wrong and going to hell.

Dr. R.: I get it. So it seems that you want your parents to go through an educational course that will get them off your back.

Client: Yeah, that would be great.

Dr. R.: Okay, and what would you be willing to do in return to earn their trust and help them to feel better about the things you are doing?

Client: Why should I have to do anything? They have the problem. I am not a drug addict, I go to school and my friends are not gangsters.

Dr. R.: In some ways you are right and I will help them to look at that, but compromise is the deal and you are going to have to meet them halfway. What are you willing to do?

Client: Well, I guess I could talk to them more about what's up. And I would be willing to let them know more about where I am and come home on time if they would be more open about how that happens.

Dr. R.: Good. Now we have something to work with. Anything else you want to let me know before I invite them back in?

Client: You are going to have to talk to them about me having a boyfriend. They think I'm too young to be dating.

Dr. R.: That is something we can discuss down the road when there is more goodwill between the three of you. Would you be willing to be responsible and accountable around this? Also, I can make suggestions, but they are your parents and they have the final say. However, if you gain some good will with them and everyone lightens up some this may be possible.

Client: Okay.

(Parents come back in.)

Dr. R.: Your daughter and I have talked. She is willing to come back and do some work on these matters. I would like it if you would take my cassette tape "Surviving Adolescence" and listen to it this week. It is an hour talk about the many components of raising a teen.

Parent: Thank you, this would be helpful.

Dr. R.: Your daughter feels that you are too strict and out of touch with regards to normal adolescents. I was quite impressed with her openness and ability to verbalize her concerns.

Parent: We are not out of touch, nor are we going to give up control and let her do what she wants to do.

Dr. R.: I never ask or expect a parent to give up their legitimate right to be a parent. However, it is not about control when you are raising a teenager. The rules about control change when a kid gets to be about eleven or twelve. It is not about control, which by design sets you up to be at war and to lose. It is about appropriate negotiation. The reason we are raising children is so that they grow up to be functioning adults. At this stage it is about helping and guiding them to make good choices and being rewarded or given consequences when they choose badly.

Parent: How do we do that?

Dr. R.: Well, compromise based on understanding all the principals' wants and feelings. From this understanding and negotiation everyone can win and your daughter learns how to attend to life before going off to college too naive to function effectively.

Parent: Okay. Is she willing to negotiate and give us what we need in order to allow her what she wants?

Dr. R.: Yes, she is.

6

Bringing Your Self To Being Male Defining Masculinity

✦

Begin With The Differences

I have suggested that men in western society are subjected to an idiosyncratic upbringing that causes them to place limits on their ability to be conscious and emotive. I do not however, think that this means that men should be excused from their actions. What I want is for both men and women to understand what being male is all about. Somehow, even with the research about gender differences, we still seem mystified. How can we better internalize the nature of gender differences? And how can we joyfully respond to them?

Many contemporary authors, such as John Gray and Robert Bly, have written about the issues of men and masculinity. I did my Ph.D. dissertation on this subject in the mid 1980's. It is an important topic that needs clarification. The questions are: What is truly masculine and what is the shadow side of masculinity? How does maleness fit into being human? And how does it apply to getting in touch with our more actualized or spiritual side of the self?

Years ago, a particular woman came into my office for psychotherapy. I asked my fateful introductory question, "Why are you here?" And she answered without hesitation, "Men are slime." I then asked her how she felt about seeing a male therapist. She said I had come highly recommended and that she would exclude me from the group for the time being. I chuckled and told her that I wished I had a dollar for every time I'd heard something to that effect from a woman client. Of course I hear similar statements from men about women, but my interest here is in getting a message across about men.

My point is not that men should do all of the changing, but we men are on an uncharted road trying to gain more substance in our lives, especially from our relationships with women. The first place for us to start is in understanding what constitutes a "guy thing." What is this manly behavior we insist upon in order to feel secure in our identity? The key to understanding the unconscious lies in the ruling force of our being, that which is in control until it is unlearned. My gut sense is that the concept of masculinity, based on self-identity and the expectation of how the world will treat us, has become a problem because "masculinity" has no universal definition and, in the truest sense, has become outdated.

Of course, there are things guys do that are more in the realm of the masculine than the feminine, and I'm not suggesting men should give these up. What I am suggesting is that we target the ways in which society teaches men to deal with situations and to deal with other people that clearly do not work. For instance, men are not encouraged to attend to the more sensitive and non-logical aspects of life, such as helping those we love feel more safe, trusted, loved, cherished, heard, included, cared for, prioritized, special, supported, partnered, and important to us.

Now, I know some of you guys who are thumbing through this book (because your wife told you to read it) might be muttering, "Oh, here's that psychobabble, wimp stuff again." My response to this is to ask you tough guys out there, what you consider to be the most important things in life? Is it your job, money, sports, cars? What about your wife or partner, your children, religion, friends, and anyone else you hold truly sacred and precious? Those people you interact with on a consistent basis make up the substance of the spiritual realm you might lightly refer to as "wimp stuff." It is these relationships that bring about the life giving qualities of caring and communication that are essential for us to be happy and whole.

The following dialogue illustrates a simple difference between men and women.

Wife: I wish he would stop and give us some time. We never spend any quality time together and we never talk.

Dr. R.: What do you think about what your wife wants?

Husband: I really don't understand it. We're together all the time.

Dr. R.: Your husband is in the dark about this.

Wife: We're together on the couch while he's watching TV and I'm reading a book, but we don't talk.

Husband: You like reading and I like TV, and besides we do talk don't we?

Wife: When, on the commercial breaks?

Husband: There are other times. Come on.

Dr. R.: Why do you think your wife feels that you don't communicate?

Husband: (exasperated) I don't know. I don't know what she wants!

Dr. R.: Why do you think your husband feels close to you even if he is watching TV?

Wife: I have no idea.

Dr. R.: This is a "Mars/Venus" thing. Men can sit together and watch a sporting event and feel like they're sharing an experience. Women need to talk and share verbally to feel connected. Men need to understand that women feel partnered for very different reasons than men. Women need to remember that when a man is hurting he goes off alone to deal with it and that men are not brought up to attend to their feelings. When stressed they need distraction, and TV is that distraction. It works for him, but it doesn't work for her.

This is the result of early learning. It is the reason all of this "guy stuff" is so ingrained in men in our society. The origins of traditional sex roles can be found in the early messages men receive during their very first years of life. Socialization theory shows us that parents and others in our social environment tend to foster differences in attitudes, behaviors, skills, and orientation in girls and boys.

Studies from my own research on men and masculinity indicate that not only are boys socialized to fit into culturally defined gender roles, but that the male role is subject to more scrutiny than the female role. R.E. Hartley, a well-known psychologist in the sixties, substantiated the idea that folk myth and social structure combine to create additional early programming of boys, stemming from a variety of reasons including the following.

a. Demands that boys conform to social notions of what is manly come much earlier and are enforced with more vigor than the same or similar attitudes with respect to girls.

b. These demands are enforced harshly, impressing the small boy with the danger of deviating from them, while he does not quite understand what they are.

c. The desired behavior is rarely defined positively as something the child should do, but rather undesirable behavior is indicated negatively as something he should not do or be. For example, he should not be a "sissy."

d. This behavior is enforced by the threats, punishment, and anger of those who are close to him.

The outcome of this cultural imperative is that boys experience an intense amount of performance anxiety due to a role model that reacts only to negative, not positive accomplishments. All too often we leave our men no alternative but to accept a role model that is nebulous at best. As early as elementary school, young males are being brought into a severely restricted cultural fold. A young boy must work to maintain the themes of power, aggression, independence, and achievement or later be labeled as less than a real man. From childhood, he must be consistently open to challenge in order to prove his masculinity and be pressured into demonstrating his skills or mastery. This is not for the praise he will receive for his actions, but so that no one will think less of him.

Exercise #1: Feeling Like a "Real Man"

Make a list of the times in your life when you remember feeling pressure to "be a man." Start with your earliest memories and bring this idea to the present. Feel free to make it a long list. Get in touch with your "manly" self. Write down your experiences of feeling like a "real man." When you are done, put your list aside for a few days and then come back to it. Do you see a common theme or thread? How have your earliest experiences of being a "real man" affected how you grew up, and who you are today?

Other studies have shown that because boys are pressured to "act like boys," they develop their identity through games or possessions earlier than girls do. By the age of two, boy children can identify items by male and female "appropriateness" with 75% accuracy. Boys are further socialized to believe that all female items are taboo, to be avoided if they are to become real men. These implied pressures to measure up to the unspoken code of the male do not apply to the same degree for girls. There is, for example, little stigma to a young girl being a tomboy, an alternative female behavior frequently indulged in without grave misgivings.

Boys however, are given explicit messages not to display any feminine behavior that threatens to earn them the derogatory label of "sissy." Girls are given more leeway to express aspects of their androgyny. And, while society would like men to be more sensitive and expressive, we are simultaneously given clear messages not to be caught dead manifesting feminine traits. For committing "unmanly" acts, we are quickly called a "wimp" or a "wuss."

I wrote earlier of the unspoken code of masculinity. One of the best descriptions of this code was presented by Warren Farrell in his 1975 book, The Liberated Male, in which he set down fifteen commandments highlighting the underlying assumptions that most boys in our culture carry with them as they enter manhood. Though first written nearly 30 years ago, these beliefs still hold true for many boys growing up today.

1. Men are biologically superior to women and therefore men have greater human potential than women.
2. Masculinity, rather than femininity, is the superior, dominant, more valued form of gender identity.
3. Masculine power, dominance, and control are essential to proving one's masculinity.
4. Vulnerabilities, feelings, and emotions in men are signs of femininity and to be avoided.
5. Masculine control of self, others, and the environment are comfortable.
6. Men seeking help and support from others show signs of weakness, vulnerability, and potential incompetence.
7. Rational and logical thought is the superior form of communication.
8. Interpersonal communications that emphasize human emotions, feelings, intuitions and physical contact are considered feminine and are to be avoided.
9. Men's success in interpersonal relations with women is contingent upon subordinating females through staying in control of the interpersonal dynamics by using power and dominance.
10. Sex is a primary means to prove one's masculinity.
11. Vulnerability and intimacy with other men are to be avoided because
    a. a man cannot be vulnerable and intimate with another man because he may be taken advantage of, and
    b. intimacy with other men may imply homosexuality or effeminacy.
12. Men's work and career success are measures of their masculinity.
13. Self-definition, self-respect, and personal worth are primarily established through achievement, success, and competence on the job.
14. Male power, control, and competition are the primary means to becoming a success and insuring personal respect, economic security, and happiness.
15. Men are vastly different and superior to women in career abilities; therefore, men's primary role is that of breadwinner or economic provider while women's primary role is that of caretaker of the home and children.

Male socialization is the way men have been reinforced to think. With this as our badge of manliness, we are by design set on a course of aggression, power, and control. If the above is the credo for most men, and we are bent on living up to the stereotype of being male, is it any wonder males have difficulty becoming conscious of how they feel or aware of the feelings of others.

Being a Different Kind of Man

Farrell's list is still relevant today. The interesting thing is that most males truly believe they do not exemplify the code. But ask them what other males think and evidence shows that many males truly believe that most men ascribe to this set of traditional standards, not so much as they interact with women but in the way they identify themselves as men. Hence, if most men believe the male species is still locked into its traditional identity, then "guy stuff" is a part of our upbringing.

For the health and well being of all, I suggest these changes in the code:

a.   Loosen up on control, power, competition, and aggression.

b.   Talk about concerns and vulnerabilities.

c.   Listen to women talk about feelings, which in turn encourages men to feel and be vulnerable.

d.   Slow down your work schedule so that:

1. Who you are is not what you do,

2. Being a provider is not the primary way to feel good about yourself and to stay in control.

e.   Don't compete with other men as a way to relate to them or to release anger.

The following dialogue represents a common form of miscommunication between men and women.

Wife: I don't like it when he gets sarcastic.

Dr. R.: What do you think about that?

Husband: Everyone does it. All my friends do it and we don't think anything of it.

Dr. R.: How does it make you feel when your husband is sarcastic?

Wife: I feel attacked and hurt.

Dr. R.: (speaking to the husband): We men are only permitted to deal with certain feelings in certain ways. Our anger is most of what we are allowed, but only in an "all or nothing" way. We are either allowed to explode or allowed to be sarcastic. Sarcasm is anger disguised as humor so that the perpetrator does not have to own the attack. There is always truth in a sarcastic remark and it is always aimed at someone. If there are a group of men and one is being sarcastic to another, there is always someone in the group who is not really laughing. And, if the targeted person does take offense the perpetrator almost always replies with one of two common comebacks; either, "Oh, I was only kidding," or, "Why are you being so sensitive?"

Dr. R.: (still speaking to the husband): What do you think of this?

Husband: I never thought of it that way.

Dr. R.: That is because this is one male accepted way to show anger.

Wife: Thank you for the explanation. This has been my experience and I don't like it.

Husband: I am sorry. This is not what I want to do to you.

Dr. R.: This is a good thing. We have to work on you being able to express your anger to your wife in a manner that makes it possible for her to hear what is not working for you.

Men cannot grow up being taught that the world will accept them only if they are able to live and compete in prescribed masculine ways and expect to dump this kind of socialization in a heartbeat. They need to learn to be men who also have many feelings. When we don't talk about our feelings, our anger is often let out through rage, competition, and sarcasm. Sarcasm, as I tell my clients, is hostility disguised as humor. This comes from years of having to grin and bear it on our own. We men are too alone. We are steeped in the credo that we must have all the answers, fix all the problems, let nothing get to us, find a way to handle it, and (my personal favorite) do it all perfectly.

As men, we need to abandon the credo and change these beliefs to allow us more of life, and of those who are in our lives. What we don't want to admit is that our reason for not changing is that we are afraid. As I say this I realize that for most men, I might as well have thrown down the gauntlet or insulted their mother. But hear me out before you take me on. How many of you have to suck it in when you think of approaching your male friends or your significant other with something deep or emotionally laden that you know will put you in a vulnerable position?

Imagine approaching a male friend, and approaching the woman in your life with your feelings and emotions. If you have no problem imagining either, my hat is off to you. As a man, you are in the minority. Most of our gender is scared senseless when it comes to these kinds of issues. We would rather face physical danger than deal with emotional exposure. Because of early training and cultural taboo, men avoid whatever brings up feelings of vulnerability. Another aspect of this fear is that men are constantly being scrutinized and evaluated by their peers. A man's standing in the club of masculinity is only as good as his last rating. And a man who braves the world of feelings is usually courting criticism.

So what needs to happen? I believe this is not so much about change as it is about the work of becoming more. And this is true for women as well. Men can be men without doing such a good job of living up to negative stereotypes.

Doesn't it seem ludicrous to ask men to put aside who they might want to be and to embrace a standard that betrays their nature? I recently read an article about fathers and sons who went to a camp in order to get away from the typical aspects of competition. There they were involved in sports without keeping score. I applaud the attempt, but give me a break. Keeping score and winning provide the passion of a sport, they are the force that makes a game exciting. Why take an all or nothing approach? "Winning" is not the problem.

The issue is how we win and how we treat the members of our own team and the other team. There is nothing wrong with one team being better that day than the other team. No matter how we cut it, we are not created equal at all times or in all things. There will always be those who are better and worse than we are. It is the attitude we have and the way we interact with those better and worse than ourselves that makes us either the good guy or the bad guy. We need to teach compassion and a healthy sense of winning, if we as men, are going to live fulfilling lives.

I have had enough of those who try to merge the male and female aspects of the self. Androgynous means having both masculine and feminine characteristics, not blending the two together. We do not need a societal welding iron that attaches these two energies. This would be like saying that people who are ambidextrous and want to be healthy or politically correct should write with both hands at the same time. The concept is laughable. A person who is ambidextrous has the luxury of doing things in one of two ways, each hand can do what it does best. This also applies to the male and female aspects of our selves. We can use our various talents where they will do the most good.

If you are in competitive sports, use your masculine side to play as well as you can. If someone is depressed or suffering, use the feminine side of yourself to be supportive and compassionate. This may seem mundane to the point of being simple, but look around. This is not happening! Because, we aren't secure enough in ourselves to know how to access these separate components of our whole self. Men especially, find little positive reinforcement beyond the rigid confines of the male stereotype, and are all too quick to tag some other guy as a "sissy." Girls may affectionately be called "tomboys," but boys get no such slack.

In the 1980's, Tom Selleck was in a weekly television drama called Magnum PI, in which his character was the heartthrob of almost every woman around. It is my contention that this occurred because the character embraced the true androgyny of his male and female sides. On the masculine side, his character was a tall, dark, handsome detective with a gun who protected women, drove a Ferrari, and was a war veteran. On the female side, he was cute, had a sense of humor, wanted to talk things out if possible, liked to communicate, and could openly express his feelings. He was a male who embraced his whole self without sacrificing his position as a man.

Well guys, this is the goal. The "homework" is what you need to do to achieve this. Of course you don't have to be the definitive androgynous male, but we need to at least start working on balancing the two sides of ourselves. If we don't attend to what we value, we run the risk of losing who we really are. In the workplace, you will be able to face the demands of commerce with the full complement of your masculine side. At home with loved ones, you can become aware of your feminine side when that is needed in order to be supportive and compassionate.

Exercise # 2: Begin a Journal

Begin a journal. Write down the emotions and feelings you experience each day. You will probably feel some resistance to doing this, but you will also find that the more you do it, the easier it will be to get in touch with your feelings and your "feminine" side. Start with, "Today I felt…" A journal is a very powerful tool, and one of the most effective ways of getting in touch with your own feelings and emotions. And the best part is that you don't have to show it to anyone.

I want to make it clear that in the real world we need all of ourselves to make this work. You need your masculine side on the job for decision-making, logic, deductive reasoning, and problem solving. However, in the workplace you are also dealing with people and their issues. In this arena, you need to understand negotiation, communication, compassion, empathy, support, compromise, and the feelings of other's. So too in the family, where we need our feminine side to express caring or to address feelings, and our masculine side to handle issues that require logic, deductive reasoning, or problem solving skills. How can men stay on the cutting edge in the workplace, with its many demands, and still relate to their families in a warm, gentle, sensitive manner? The answer is that we can't, not without a great deal of work to balance all of who we are.

Men will find it difficult to find the balance of androgyny if collectively we don't get off the back of masculinity. Men should be able to have both their muscles and their feelings without suffering emotional blackmail. Boys must be given the leeway to win at sports while also being allowed to cry when they feel the need to cry. Let's end the scrutiny of boys and men under the microscope of humanity. Parents, especially fathers, need to stop worrying about their sons turning out to be "real" men. When the doctor delivers your child and proclaims, "It's a boy!" he is telling you that the child already is a "real male." Boys can't get any more real than the penis they are born with. The job of fathers and mothers is to teach and mold their sons to be good, decent, strong, reality oriented, caring individuals who know the difference between right and wrong. Teach your sons to be cognizant of ways to balance their masculine and feminine sides without feeling ashamed of either. In order for you to accomplish this you will have to believe in it yourself and confidently model these qualities and abilities.

How does a man stretch so far as to embrace a part of himself that he has been taught to be ashamed of? The fear of being a sissy is deep seeded in our culture and is initiated at the onset of male understanding. A man must reach down into his gut, to his very soul, to come up with the makings of androgyny. But what could possibly motivate a man to do this? For he must first want to do it in order to achieve it.

Reasons to Believe in Change

I have outlined many good reasons to want to change. One's own sense of peace and contentment, a desire to be whole, a desire to have the drama end in exchange for an easier way of being, and a desire for relationships to be more fulfilling are all reasons to embrace these ideas. Additionally, it could be that fathers do not want their sons to experience the same limitations their masculinity has imposed on them. What matters is that you choose to be more, to go beyond your socialization of what a man "should be," to discover for yourself what kind of person you can be.

The next step is to find a vehicle, a mentor, teacher, or a path that can take you down the road away from your own prejudices and insecurities. This means you will to have to confront the shadows and questions of your inner child. What do you feel makes you a "real man?" What is your bottom line sense about being a human being? Men need to take their heads out of the sand; notice that their marriages are not particularly happy; see that their teenagers have too much anger, aggression, or withdrawal; recognize that their daughters are too shy, too thin, or too needy; and fess up to the fact that everyone around them is either guarded or in pain. Men must do the courageous thing, step up to the plate and take a good hard look at what is going on in their families. Then they can listen without trying to fix everything and "make it all okay." The old road takes a lot of unlearning. You need a good guide to point things out to you as you go forward on this new and sometimes frightening path.

In this process as in all things, who you are and how you validate yourself is known only from the inside out. We have been taught to view the outside as a reference point, and that the best measure of who we are is to compare and contrast ourselves to others. But this standard does nothing to enhance the self. In fact, it facilitates a weak and unempowered perspective, regardless of one's gender. From this perspective, the most that can be achieved is a momentary reprieve from the inner dread that one doesn't measure up. In the writing the "Desiderata" it says that this, "will only cause you to be vain or bitter."

Your point of power resides in the center of your being and concerns who you are and what your truth is. A man has a penis and he has a heart. These alone really are enough to qualify us as men, and as human beings with the capacity to feel. We need only do the challenging and courageous work of owning ourselves, not based on the insecure and unstable reference points of stereotypes, outside validations, or name calling, but from an independent center most often referred to as the inner self.

Our sense of who we know ourselves to be as men, and more globally as human beings, need not twist and turn like leaves blowing in the wind. We can be as solid as a rock. With our self as the anchor we can be secure. The old saying "stand like a man" is an ambiguous, outdated reference point perpetuating poor self worth, a lack of confidence, and a wavering sense of security. Instead, "stand like a complete human being." Be the whole self you can be and manifest independently the best of both your masculine and feminine self. This will lead you to a clear and definitive portrayal of each gender, optimally integrated into a whole, complete and fulfilled self.

Section III:

The Benefits

✦

7

Mastering The Ego

✦

Fame or Integrity, which is more important?
Money or Happiness, which is more valuable?
Success or Failure, which is more destructive?
If you look to others for fulfillment,
You will never truly be fulfilled.
If your happiness depends on money,
You will never be happy yourself.
Be content with what you have,
Rejoice in the way things are.
When you realize that there is nothing lacking,
The whole world belongs to you.

—Lao Tzu

Letting Go

After healing the wounds of the ego, the next step is to let go of the now complete and healthy ego to enable you to remember the essence of your true earthly being. It is that essential being which reflects who you really are. Only when you are in touch with your true being can you begin to summon the potential of all you are and only then can you accomplish all you are here to accomplish. To let go of the ego, to get out of your own way, and to solidify the self is the absolute goal of psychotherapy.

When you were born, you were endowed with the collective unconscious; the totality of human essence, perhaps even including the lessons you learned from many previous lifetimes. The collective unconscious, this Jungian term refers to a cellular library that holds the totality of mankind's experienced knowledge. In the Hindu culture this is called the "Atman" or collective knowing of all mankind. These vast information banks are tucked away in the deepest regions of every human being, available to those who do the work and are able to get out of their own way. Each of us has the potential to regain this knowledge, but most people never find the discipline and the courage it takes to sit with their demon shadow and discover the vast resources of knowledge and light within.

The following dialogue illustrates the confusion many of us feel about this.

Client: I'm not sure who I am.

Dr. R.: What do you mean?

Client: I am so locked into what everyone wants from me. I'm always checking out how someone else sees me and what it is they expect of me.

Dr. R.: Tell me where and when this shows up.

Client: Everywhere and always.

Dr. R.: If you are always concerned with the expectations of others, how can you know who you are?

Client: Right.

Dr. R.: What you are describing is what I call "being a chameleon." You are always changing who you are to match the person you are with. It turns out that you are never the same, even with yourself. There was a movie out called Runaway Bride. In this movie Julia Roberts plays a woman behaving as a chameleon, attempting to fit into the life of her fiancé at the time. Richard Gere plays a journalist who helps her to see this and to find herself.

Client: I have seen that, but I'll rent it again. I really want to understand this. I have never looked at myself this way, but it makes perfect sense.

Dr. R.: Yes! You are always looking outside of you to the other person's needs and likes, without paying attention to yourself. Therefore, thinking about yourself is going against your habit.

Client: Well...okay, now that we have that figured out what's next?

Dr. R.: If only it were that simple. Your head now has an intellectual understanding of the work that we need to do. Our work however, is to discover from whom you learned this belief system and to deal with the feeling state around it.

Client: Somehow I didn't think it would be that easy.

Dr. R.: You were right.

This tangible essence within is able to manifest when we realize we are more than we think. As our fears begin to lessen and their influence on our psyche diminishes, a new experience of self can be embraced. Nevertheless, you might be apprehensive about such an unfamiliar and uncharted endeavor. Perhaps you will feel that because your newfound "Self" feels so good, it cannot last. It can take a while to accept the sense of more self, to know we are not becoming someone else but rather awakening to a deeper and more complete sense of who we truly are.

Being All You Can Be

In his 1994 inaugural speech, Nelson Mandela illuminates this point with this thoughtful expression of self:

> Our deepest fear is not that we are inadequate.
> Our deepest fear is that we are powerful beyond measure.
> It is our light, not our darkness, that most frightens us.
> We ask ourselves, "Who am I to be brilliant, gorgeous,
> talented and fabulous?"
> Actually, who are you not to be?
> You are a child of God.
> Your playing small doesn't serve the world.
> There is nothing enlightened about shrinking so that other
> people won't feel insecure around you.
> We were born to manifest the glory of God that is
> within all of us.
> It is not just in some of us: it's in everyone.
> And as we let our own light shine, we unconsciously
> give other people permission to do the same.
> As we are liberated from our own fears, our presence
> automatically liberates others.

Think about the many times you held back in fear of being all you can be and how you worried about what others were thinking. We learn in childhood that we should not take the light from others. And it is also true that at first we are afraid we truly might be our darkest shadow. As we get older, being afraid has to do with whether or not we might actually be inadequate. We mistakenly think it's better not to take a risk.

Think about the last time you succeeded at something and were rewarded for what you had done. Do you remember feeling that your strengths were too visible and that someone around you might have a problem with who you were becoming? Teenagers learn to hide good grades so that those who are "cool" won't shun them. Adults who have a lot of money often hide the fact from their friends and neighbors. If they don't, they may become the object of jealousy. I remember a colleague who, after she had written a book, told me she was grateful for my congratulations because her other friends were having trouble with her new status in life.

Mr. Mandela is right. It serves no one to "shrink" our selves so that others will feel more at ease. It is the insecurity of the ego that causes this shrinking when it begins comparing us to others around us, seeking to validate our worth from the outside, instead of from within.

It is a great joy to be liberated from the need for outside validation. To know inside, with absolute certainty, that we were born to "manifest the glory of God that is within all of us" is one of the greatest gifts this life has to offer. It is a gift we can give ourselves when we get out of our own way. Do the work. Look for the light within. You will find the negative effects of others, who might judge you, fall away like autumn leaves in a strong breeze.

Exercise # 1: Just Imagine

Sit quietly with paper and pen. Imagine your self as you would be if you had moved beyond all your fears and worries about what others might think of you. Describe your self. How do you look? How do you stand? How do you move? Where are you? What is your expression? What are you doing? What can you accomplish with your life that you couldn't accomplish before?

8

Embracing Empowerment

✦

Reframing is the Idea of Power.
Knowing others is intelligence,
knowing yourself is true wisdom.
Mastering others is true strength,
mastering yourself is true power...

—Lao Tzu

Reclaiming Your Power Within

We don't acquire power. We reclaim power. We are born with our power, then willingly give it up through submission to our parents in exchange for our very survival.

Before going further, let me make some distinctions about what it is I mean by 'power' and empowerment. In Western society, power generally means control over others and the acquisition of material wealth, especially in a capitalistic sense. The word 'power' seldom refers to the inner strength, centeredness and subtle energy the Chinese call the 'chi.' Instead, we use the word 'power' to describe the ego state in which your feet are planted firmly on the necks of those around you. It's the *He who dies with the most toys wins* mentality. It's about vanity, the constant struggle for acquisition and control, winning and losing, and keeping score. It's what is meant by the "dark side of the force" in the movie Star Wars.

Empowerment better describes the real and genuine internal power each of us possesses. It is "the force" itself, and can be used by each of us to control our personal destiny and to make things happen in our lives. Ideally, when we manifest and create what we choose to have in our lives we do so from a position of inner strength and respect. When we do this we serve as a model, inviting others to share in our success and to emulate it if they choose. It is not a win-lose perspective but a win-win point of view. Empowerment is a concept independent of clichés, one that challenges us to be whole and complete.

From the Tao Te Ching:

> When the Master governs, the people
> are hardly aware that he exists.
> Next best is the leader who is loved.
> Next is one who is feared.
> The worst is one who is despised.
> If you don't trust the people,
> you make them untrustworthy.
> The Master doesn't talk, he acts.
> When the work is done,
> the people say, "Amazing!
> We did it all by ourselves!"

To feel empowered is the very foundation of confidence, compassion, strength, and mastery. It is the ability to be all you can be without giving up any part of yourself, and without inviting attack or ridicule even though you are open and vulnerable. Many people cannot imagine a way to be vulnerable and also to be safe. But when you know who you are, combining the strength of your intellect with open and genuine feelings enables you to share your true self completely and to remain totally safe. Conversely, when we are locked into more typical Western power thinking, we lose sight of this inner strength that allows us to be overtly vulnerable yet immune to attack.

In our feeling-denied society, those who have not done their self-work are at the mercy of anyone who catches them expressing their feelings. It is painfully obvious that when you are not in touch with your feelings, others can take advantage of you. Conversely, when you truly own your feelings, rarely will others be able to push you off balance. For example, if someone complains that you are slow to get the point, you can agree without losing yourself or giving up control. You can respond simply by speaking a truth about yourself. "Yes, I know that, but I make up for it in the depth of my understanding." Or, "I can see why you would say that. You know, I think it will work better for both of us if I get back to you on this."

When you share something sensitive or even painful from a place of empowerment, it doesn't matter whether the recipient is empathetic or not. This type of power has nothing to do with giving up yourself to others or to their attack on you. If a person shows any sign of disrespect, you become aware of it, and simply discontinue what you are saying, thus setting your own limits and setting back your antagonist. It is disempowering to believe that an open, sharing person is somehow at the mercy of another. No one can make you feel what you do not choose to feel. The only choice you can make is whether to turn over your power, or not. When you have done the work and live within a strong sense of yourself, your way is clear, safe, and balanced.

When someone makes a negative comment that is a put down without any basis to it, you do not have to own it but can instead say to your antagonist, "That is not how I see myself, and I certainly don't agree with what you just said." Someone who is cognizant of their true self is not taken by surprise by such an attack. They own their actions in an empowered way and the surprise is thrown back on the attacker. In most cases, this leaves the aggressor speechless, and anxious to move away. Your empowerment acts as an impenetrable shield.

Without a strong sense of empowerment, it is easy to cave into such put downs: losing eye contact, stammering, lowering your head, changing the tone of your voice, shifting weight, looking around for a way out, or feeling ridiculously awkward. When this happens you are feeling the affects of turning over your power. You have moved one notch down in the game called "I'm not in touch with who I am." Or, "I am feeing insecure and you just caught me." Thus you experience a sense of loss because the other person has used your unawareness against you. This can never happen when you are in touch with your feelings and know with certainty who you really are.

The following dialogue exemplifies the way this feels.

Client: I feel like I have no power.

Dr. R.: Where do you see yourself turning over your power?

Client: Everywhere. It seems like everyone has more ability to get what they want than I do.

Dr. R.: Give me an example of where, and to whom, you lose your power.

Client: For instance, I talk to my husband and no matter what I say, he debates it until I give up. Even when I feel very strong about it, sooner or later I give up.

Dr. R.: What do you think happens that you let him have power over you?

Client: I'm not sure. I feel like he knows more than I do. In fact, I feel like most people know more than I do. Also, I feel that somehow no one believes me and I have to explain myself all the time.

Dr. R.: You mean you have to prove and justify yourself to everyone.

Client: That is exactly what I mean.

Dr. R.: So you not only don't know you are creditable, but you have no idea you are worthwhile enough to be taken seriously and listened to.

Client: Yep, that's me.

Dr. R.: And consequently, you don't hold your own in conflict and you don't know that you have the tools you need to go into battle.

Client: Yes, pitiful isn't it.

Dr. R.: Not pitiful, sad. It is sad that you have learned that you are not worthy enough to be listened to, heard, and valued. We have some work to do.

Client: What do you mean exactly?

Dr. R.: Well, we have to help you unlearn by finding the origins of your belief that you are not all the things I just mentioned. You have been taught to give up your power and not to have faith in yourself. We need to change this belief. This is doable and we will get there, but it needs to be done.

Client: Okay, when do we start?

Dr. R.: We already have.

No one Can Make You Feel Inferior Without Your Consent

I often tell my clients that the only way to win is not to play. Because someone throws down the gauntlet does not mean you have to pick it up. To play someone else's game is to give them your power. What follows is an example of refusing to play someone else's game.

At the end of a consulting job I did with a corporate group, the CEO of the company came up to me to express his thanks for all I had contributed in the session. However, in his own way he also needed to let me know that he was still in control. And because he didn't know how to appropriately communicate this mixture of emotions, he hit me verbally with a sarcastic comment.

Sarcasm is a way of putting down another person, or even one's self, by using humor to disguise anger or hostility. Then, if called on the remark, the offender will most likely respond by questioning the self-esteem of the offended person, "Don't be so sensitive! I was only kidding," or "What's the matter, can't you take a joke?" are common responses. But the reality is that there is nothing funny about sarcasm and someone always gets the brunt of sarcastic remarks. The person who is the object of sarcasm seldom laughs with everyone else, and never for the same reasons.

When you are in touch with your feelings you are much more likely to perceive an intended attack for what it is, no matter how subtle. In the previous example, when the CEO used sarcasm in his reference to my contribution, instead of coming back at him with sarcasm of my own, I looked right at him and said, "Ouch!" He was totally caught by surprise. He looked as if he had just realized he was stepping on my foot and asked, "What happened?" I called the process by asking him, "Did you *mean* to put me down with that remark?" He looked even more surprised, mumbled "no," and walked away.

Exercise # 1: Responding to Sarcasm

Over the next few days notice at least five situations in which you or someone else is the victim of a sarcastic remark or verbal barb. There are thousands of examples on television every night. Write down these examples and then sample empowered responses for each situation. Practice saying them out loud.

When you call an attacker on the reality of what they have just done, they have two choices. They can address the process or they can walk away from it. Either way, there is no need for you to attack or belittle anyone in your response. It is possible to take care of your self without being disrespectful, and to be sure the aggressor will not be successful if they continue with the attack. If they do continue, you continue to address the process. For example, if the CEO had persisted in his attack, I could have continued to remain in control of my sense of self, and clearly set limits by saying something like, "As a professional businessman I am sure you know the value of relationships based on trust and mutual respect. I am also sure you'd never want to do anything that would be disrespectful of another nor would you intentionally create an atmosphere of distrust. Now, what was it you meant to say to me?"

Another example of this happened at a party I was attending with a former girlfriend of mine. We were standing around when a friend of hers came over. At some point in the conversation this third person made a sarcastic remark directed at me. I responded to her just as I had to the CEO by saying, "Ouch!" Startled and surprised, she actually stepped back, looking down to see if she had stepped on my foot. When she looked up I asked, "Did you mean to put me down by what you said?" She turned a deep shade of red and quickly walked away mumbling to herself, "not really…" My companion smiled thoughtfully and said, "That was the quickest disarming of her I have ever seen." The woman was a habitual sarcastic and my former girlfriend had been a nervous witness and sometime victim of her verbal barbs. Now she knew how to better deal with her in the future.

The reason most antagonistic people walk away when confronted honestly is because their sense of self is not aligned with who they have just put themselves out to be. They do not have the courage or insight to own their remarks. I became vulnerable when I let these people know I was feeling attacked, but I was not about to turn my power or safety over to them in the process. When you are clear about your strengths and your limitations, no one can get to you. The key is standing up for who you are and knowing your limits around what affects you. The challenge is becoming completely conscious and secure about who you are and what you are willing to own about yourself. You can do this when you walk in your truth, work with and honor yourself, and know that your words have merit. In this way, you will find you are not open to any type of negative recourse, no matter how persistent your antagonist.

Taking Ownership

> She who is centered in the Tao
> Can go where she wishes, without danger.
> She perceives the Universal Harmony,
> Even amidst great pain,
> Because she has found peace in her heart.
> —Lao Tzu

Owning who we are in relation to the way others see us is an important part of reclaiming our power. For some people, this sense of "ownership" is confusing because ownership is usually thought of in terms of possession of material objects. We are not accustomed to the idea of ownership in regard to our feelings and behavior. Perhaps the word "responsibility" is more familiar, but adult reality is already too bogged down in responsibility. The word "ownership" better captures our attention. To own something is intriguing, it connotes self-control as well as a positive sense of self-possession.

To understand ownership, we must be absolutely clear about who we are and who we are not. This more often than not entails recognizing something we may have overlooked, the fact that we are all imperfectly human. Society is obsessively focused on perfection, being perfect and looking perfect. This dis-empowering process catches the unwary in the "should" and "should not" thinking that causes us to be less than all we can be. Having to always "look good" keeps us trapped into thinking we must deny the very nature of ourselves. For many, imperfection is a horrible reality. Burnout, chronic fatigue, anxiety, sleep disorders, and depression are but a few symptoms that are a direct result of our need for perfection. Our society is littered with the psychic remains of those who thought they had all the answers, could fix all the problems, needed no time to think things over, never said they didn't know, and clearly never needed help.

Many women joke about men who never ask for directions. But in fact, most men do not even admit to being lost. They are "temporarily unsure of their location." All of us, men and women, have been taught from childhood to avoid our imperfections, mistakes and our incompetence. Society's demand for perfection implies that we will be held back, punished for, and made lesser than others by our imperfections. A very important and significant aspect of the self-work that lies ahead, and a key aspect of true empowerment, lies in the concept of owning our imperfection. If you hold yourself to a standard of perfection, your work is to uncover the origins of this standard. Once you realize you do not have to be perfect, you will learn to be easier on yourself and you will gain clarity about who you really are.

Exercise # 2: Stop Relinquishing Your Power

Think of someone in your life to whom you give up your power. Discover the roots of your behavior by looking for all of the "should" and "should not" thinking patterns embedded in your inner dialogue as it relates to this person. What are the messages you get from them that take away your power? How could you better respond in a way that empowers you and is respectful to them?

Another selective pitfall is ignorance! Are you ever afraid of being called stupid? Do you worry that someone may find out that you cannot rise to the occasion (sound familiar guys)? Why? Do we really think we have to know it all? Why is it unacceptable to be ignorant about something and why is it not okay to be able to admit to it without being labeled a "wus"? For example, I know nothing about car engines. I choose to stay ignorant of the inner workings of the automobile and I let the experts do their job when it comes to fixing and working on my car. As a guy, I'm supposed to know at least something about fixing cars, especially if I run across a woman in automobile distress. But if this happens, I will take out my handy cell phone and call roadside service to come to take care of her car problem.

If someone chooses to make fun of the fact that I know nothing about fixing cars, I just look them in the eye and say, "Yep, that's right" And that is that. I do not question what kind of guy I am and what others will think of me. I am willing to accept that I am ignorant in this area. If I truly wanted to know something about fixing cars, I could take a class or research the subject on the Internet. But personally, I choose not to do this because I choose to put my energy elsewhere. I can accept what I do not know because I have made a conscious choice about what I choose to know, and this serves me on a much higher level.

Exercise # 3: The Need for Perfection

Think of three situations in your life in which you feel the need to be perfect, when you have to "know it all" or "do it all." Now, think of them one by one and form a statement about each. For example, "I feel I need to have perfect patience with my kids." Now, in a very simple, loving matter of fact tone, say to your self, "I don't have perfect patience with my kids." Repeat this several times, accepting it more and more about yourself each time you say it. Realize this is the truth and that you can safely admit to it. Do this for each situation.

When you truly know who you are, you are fully empowered and invulnerable to attack. No one can take away your power. It is only when you mistakenly believe that someone or something outside of you is necessary for your validation that you lose your power and become vulnerable. It is only when we get locked into "should" and "should not" thinking that we are at the mercy of others. To be empowered is to be conscious of the reality of who you are. By being all of who you are, you remain clear and balanced, and at the mercy of no one.

9

Demystifying the Boogeyman

✦

Weapons are the tools of fear;
A decent man will avoid them
Except in the direst necessity
And, if compelled, will use them
Only with the utmost restraint.
Peace is the highest value.
If the peace has been shattered,
How can he be constant?

—Lao Tzu

Fearlessness on the Path to Love

Fear keeps us from learning our life lessons and enjoying the reality of who we are. Fear is the single most disarming aspect of life and fear is the basis, if not the cause, of all our self-sabotage. If we are going to get out of our own way, we have to let go of fear and live in our truth. To discover our essence, we must step out of the darkness of fear and into the light of love. It is only when we put fear behind us that we can walk our path and learn our life lessons.

I have a friend and colleague who shared with me a wonderful insight. Over lunch one day in the midst of an otherwise casual conversation, he bestowed upon me a profound sense of reality. It was around something I had previously read about and heard about, but this time there was something different in the way I received it that brought the truth home. What he told me was that most people are mistaken in their belief that love and hate are opposites, and that this is not at all the case. The opposite of love is fear. I later learned that this understanding comes from the work of Jerry Jampolsky.

In order to achieve the ultimate joy of love and trust, we must first let go of fear and then trust our heart. Then, a loving feeling takes over that is far beyond the mundane sense of love; this is the love that transcends opposites. I remember pointing out to my colleague that this is the God love or Buddha love we read about, meditate on, or hear about in our religious services.

But if you let it, fear can take you off of any path you are on, be it personal or spiritual. Fear is the one emotion that puts you right back into the panic of the child, feeling frightened and unable to protect yourself. Most often this fear has no basis in reality, yet it can grasp anyone at anytime. Like little ones in the night, sure that the boogeyman is out there somewhere, just waiting. When fear gets its chokehold on us it is very hard to get free from it.

When the world seems full of dark and evil, the only way out is to take hold of one's self, look around, and change perspectives. What I mean by this is that when we take stock of our surroundings, things are rarely as out of hand as we are projecting. Released from our panic, we can take a deep breath and examine what it was that set us off. And from this perspective we can work on solutions and regain our state of empowerment. Only when we release our fears will we be able to get back into the heart and feel our center. And it is only from the place of the heart that we can move forward. This is the place of quiet, where intuition, wisdom, and knowledge have a chance to surface and assist us.

Insecurity, rejection, abandonment, thrill, success and abundance all have a fear threshold. At the extreme, the ultimate fear is death and the perceived aloneness that it brings. If we could overcome the fear of death by realizing that we are never truly alone, that we are the spirit within, then the heights from which we could fly would be limitless. Franklin Roosevelt said, "We have nothing to fear but fear itself." Truer words were never spoken. In essence, once again this speaks to the purpose and the goal of emotional fitness.

Have you ever sat down and looked at what you are most afraid of? Have you truly taken stock of how many times the things you feared the most never happened? Has it dawned on you how much energy you put into avoiding your fears? Now is an excellent time to take a personal inventory of just how often that which you fear has actually shown up to chase you down.

Exercise #1: Zapping Negative Energy

Think of a situation that causes you to feel anxious, one that creates negativity for you. As you think of yourself in that situation imagine a white light surrounding you. Watch as the white light magically attracts all of the negative energy from the situation, "zapping" it into non-existence. After you've done this, take a moment to get in touch with what is in your heart. Have your feelings about the situation changed? The next time you are actually in that situation in your life, remember to use your light negative energy zapper."

A New Perspective on Fear

The actual manifestation of your fears brings about a self-prophesying "I told you so!" When you turn your back on what most frightens you and don't face your fears, they can take you from the molehill to the mountain. The lack of courage to name your fear will almost certainly harm you on some level. Fear and the energy that goes with it will run you into the ground because they gather force and momentum when you don't deal with them, draining your energy as you procrastinate, fret about your future, and avoid doing what needs to be done in the here and now. The very things you believe will keep your fears at bay (denial, rationalization, flight) are what actually give them strength and life.

We must do our emotional work by dealing with our fears. Sometimes this involves a leap of faith, a belief that there is a higher power, and that we truly are not left on our own to confront our fears and to name our shadow side. It also takes great courage to accept that family, friends, mentors, teachers, and therapists are all available to us. We should be grateful when our fears arise. It is at this time that we are most alive and have the greatest potential for growth. Deepak Chopra has been quoted as saying, "I ask for all the uncertainty that the day can bring me."

It is during these times of uncertainty that we rely on our intellect, our creativity and our courage to meet the tasks before us. I believe Dr. Chopra sees uncertainty as a way of challenging himself to bring all of who he is to the party of life. We all do this to some extent in order to stay sharp and to feel truly alive. It keeps us on our toes, and allows us to confront our fears and to learn the lessons in life we are actually here to learn. This could be considered part of the process of emotional fitness.

If we truly believe that avoiding and suppressing our fears is the key to making them go away, we will miss a lot. In reality, the very opposite brings resolve, closure and strength. Think about it. Does the Bible say, "Yea, though I walk through the valley of death I will fear no evil (because I have alcohol, drugs, denial, adultery, and gluttony as my companions)?" No. I fear no evil because, "Thou art with me; Thy rod and Thy staff comfort me." The valley of the shadow of death represents the core level of fear. The Bible does not say to walk around, bypass or jump over the valley. The Bible says to "walk through" the valley. The psychotherapeutic term for this is to "emotional work" or "process."

I'm sure I have friends who will read this and chuckle to themselves because they know that I've had a great deal of fear in my life. It is part of the lesson I am here to learn—to have faith and to work through my fears. Like many of you, I've had to walk through some horrendous trials. In that these lessons didn't kill me, they made me stronger and have allowed me to look back and say, "Thank God, this is behind me now and I am still alive." In order to survive difficult times with any modicum of sanity, I tell myself, "This is not the end of the world, and I *will* make it through!" I express my faith knowing this is a lesson like others I have lived through and that there will be more to come. I might still be hanging on for dear life, but I have a pretty good sense that my intuition is correct and a faith that keeps me solid and safe. I know that I must allow my spirit to support my emotional side, which sometimes wants to run off screaming into the night.

Even in the worst of my fear-based nightmares, I remember the world is an illusion set up for my enlightenment. Nonetheless, it often takes all my energy and focus to keep my faith in the forefront of my thoughts. I have to remember that there is a destiny, that these trials too will pass and that I will be so much more for having had the experience. Many a tough moment has actually given way to insight and wisdom. But those who refuse to learn from the hard times are left to experience them again and again. In these situations, fear becomes the antagonist one is trying to beat-up or overcome in all the wrong ways. And typically, we continue to run in many different ways that continue to cause confusion and chaos.

The following dialogue illustrates just one of the many ways in which fear can affect our lives.

Client: I get anxious and feel unable to complete the tasks I have set for myself.

Dr. R.: How does the anxiety manifest itself?

Client: I get scared. My heart pounds. I feel like I can't bring myself to the task and I withdraw or get busy with things that don't matter.

Dr. R.: What scares you most about completing these tasks?

Client: I feel like I can't do them well enough or right enough.

Dr. R.: What is the right way?

Client: I don't really know. It seems that there must be a way of completing them that is the only way to do it. I always feel like I don't get it. Like I just don't know the secret.

Dr. R.: What do you think others know that you don't know?

Client: They seem to have the tools and the truth about how to go about things that I just did not get somehow.

Dr. R.: You're holding onto the belief that you are inferior, and every time you step up to attend to something your unconscious fear sets in and you freeze.

Client: Yeah, that is how it feels. I have great intentions of accomplishing something and somehow I get afraid or distracted and never complete it. It's as if I'm like a child, too small and inadequate to really get it done.

Dr. R.: Your conscious, healthy self knows you can do the job, but the unconscious sense of yourself is sure it cannot succeed. So you start a project with the appropriate intentions of your healthier self but then your unconscious sabotages the effort.

Client: That's exactly what happens. I feel good as I begin, but I end up feeling so defeated at the end. It makes me crazy and really depressed.

Dr. R.: I understand. You have these skills that you want to use, but something gets in the way and the pattern of defeat occurs once again. This is called an introject. It is when you do to your self what was done to you as you were growing up. Many of my patients have had an overbearing parent who was so controlling and domineering that no matter what they started the parent often came in and took it over. This creates anxiety and a sense of inferiority, a belief that you can never do it "right." Right, according to the introject, is when your parents' intrusion into what you were doing sent a message to your self-esteem that you are not able and skilled enough to do it in the fashion that your parent's perfectionism demanded.

Client: My father was like that. Almost every time I began a project he would have to come in and show me how it "should" be done. I remember feeling dejected and stupid. It even got to the place where I would refuse to build something with him for fear that he would end up making me feel wrong and inadequate.

Dr. R.: Hence the fear you have of starting something and the sabotage before completion. We now have more foundation issues that were set into your belief system stating that you are unable to do it right. Now that we have the name of this learning we can go after the unlearning of it. Faith in one's self cannot exist if one has fear about one's own abilities.

The only beneficial way to attend to your fears is to stand your ground and let the Universe know you are firm in your resolve. Every time there is fear, or even panic, send it up to that "energy fly zapper in the sky." In this way, negative thoughts are taken out of your existence and you can have peace. The problem is that some negative thoughts are really persistent. You may have to send a recurring thought up to the white light many times before it is truly released. But I know that if you stay on top of any negativity as often as it comes up, you will begin to feel a greater peace as you realize the heavy energy drain is gone and you feel lighter and happier.

I heard a rumor that Wayne Dyer alleviates negative thoughts simply by saying to himself, "Next!" I would love to ask him how many times it takes for one negative thought to go away. The point is that there are many different ways to let go of negativity. The important thing is to make it go away. We have all had those moments when our emotions were so rattled with anxiety that we couldn't find the words to express our feelings. The overwhelming upset we experience at such times cripples us to the point of not being able to successfully use our faculties. We are unable to flow with the situation. When we allow our fear to handcuff us our essence cannot manifest in all its glory. Only when our fear level is down can we put our feet on the path. When we deal with our fears, the overwhelming fog of fear lifts and our vision is clear.

The Power of Naming
The Tao that can be told
Is not the eternal Tao
The name that can be named
Is not the eternal Name.
The unnamable is the eternally real.
Naming is the origin
Of all particular things.

—Lao Tzu

We need to work through our fears and to name them in order to work through them. I often say to clients that to give a name to that which haunts us is to take away its power. Naming is the act of bringing into the light the specific nature of whatever has a hold on you. If you were to describe someone who frightens you, would it give you peace of mind to know that this person is medium height, medium build, brown hair and fair skinned with brown eyes? My guess is that this would not be enough. You'd want to know more specific information about this person, such as his name and address. Without a name, the unconscious undercurrents cause us our biggest fears and trigger acting-out behavior. Bringing these unconscious undercurrents to the surface and naming them is fundamental to the work.

Exercise # 2: Naming Our Fears

Think of something in your life you've always wanted to do or to stop doing, but have had continual trouble accomplishing. Weight loss, exercise programs, spiritual practices, putting yourself on a budget, breaking a bad habit, sticking up for yourself, giving a speech, anything that requires you to get out of your own way. Think of the moment you realize you are about to "go off" into the behavior you would prefer to stop. Get in touch with your feelings at that moment. It is important that this moment is just before you actually go off, like when you've opened the refrigerator door and you're about to reach for something you know you shouldn't eat. What are the feelings at that moment in time just before you "lose it?" Name them. Anything. It doesn't matter, whatever name first pops into your head. The next time you find yourself with those feelings, name them again. Simply say, "hello feelings" and name them. After you've done this a few times, it's quite likely you will find there has been a shift in your behavior.

The bottom line fear is abandonment, the feeling of being lost and alone. To children, abandonment is death, a foreboding sense of death. The unconscious mind is created from birth through about eight years of age. This unconscious creation is the core cellular sense of who we are and how the world sees us. When there is abandonment, the child experiences emptiness instead of a flow of self-esteem and self-confidence. In adulthood, this feels like a cavern that needs to be filled, too often with alcoholism, drug abuse, overeating, and other forms of dysfunctional behavior.

As our underlying feelings are triggered and because we have not named them, we find we are at the mercy of our fears. This shows up as an inner sense of panic, perhaps causing extreme agitation or even terror. It can feel as though your insides are restless and you have a strong need and an intense craving to get or do something, anything. This something almost always is not good for you. It could be as simple as eating sweets, or it might be as extremely sabotaging as substance abuse.

When we are being chased by our unnamed demons, we truly run. There seems to be no way to turn off the palpitation deep down in our gut. And what makes matters worse is that because we have not named it, the discomfort level increases in size with each step we take in our effort to out run it. The more we try to get away, the more this panic feeds our fear. It is only by naming this shadow that we can bear to stand in our own tracks and summon up the courage it takes to deal with it. Only when we know the name by which it holds onto our psyche can we stand up to it. Doing this takes tremendous presence of mind and will. We are in fact challenging our core fears around death.

The next time you experience fear, panic, or even physical cravings, and you know you shouldn't act on them, try merely sitting still with yourself. I doubt that you will sit for very long if you don't know the name of what is attacking you. You may even find you are helpless to fend off the compulsive need to act out.

Exercise # 3: Letting Go of Fear

Think of a situation in which your fear held you back. There are probably hundreds of examples from your teen years; but try to pick a situation that is more recent. Now, imagine you are back in that situation and you are absolutely in control of your fears. See yourself acting in the situation without the fear. How did it come out differently? Is this something you'd like to have all the time? The first step in overcoming our fears is to know who they are (naming them), and second, to know when to let go of our fears because the price we pay is much too high if we continue to hang onto them. If this exercise is less than effective for you, perhaps the price you are paying isn't high enough. If this is the case, go ahead and imagine what will happen if you keep your fear for five more years, ten more years, the rest of your life! Then repeat the exercise.

The role of faith cannot be overestimated in facing our fears. We live in a tangible and pragmatic world and if you haven't been given faith you will have to work for it. Like anything new, you have to create the newness and walk with it for a lot of miles before it is a habit. It's not "seeing is believing," it's more like believing is seeing. You have to hold an intention of the possibility of faith before there can be faith. Faith deals with fears and dialogues with your fears, keeping you on your path. Faith and friends aren't tested in the good times. They're tested in the bad times.

In Ursula K. Le Guin's The Furthest Shore, the first book is about naming monsters. If you can name the monsters even dragons can be tamed. Don't put a title on your fear, "my wife," or "my husband" or "my boss." The names you give your fears come from inside of you. These people poke something inside of you. But the process is inside of you and that is where you need to go to name your fears.

The internal names of our fears are usually predicated on the bottom line psychological fear of abandonment, along with insecurity, low self esteem, fear of rejection, not being liked or good enough, inadequacy, a sense of being a fraud and last but not least the feeling of being unacceptable so that we don't want to let anyone get too close for fear that they will come to see the real us.

When fear chases you down it grows in power. You give it power by running. It feeds off your running. That's why alcoholism and substance abuse spiral ever upward in destructiveness. They feed off your fears and your fears make it worse and worse until it consumes you. But this is not a natural or necessary way to live. By naming your fears, "calling them out," and taming them, you can begin to discover the simple joys of claiming your essence within.

10

Exploring The Inner Caverns Becoming Clear

✦

I honor those who try
To rid themselves of lying,
Who empty the self,
And have only clear being there.

—Rumi

What is important to you lives within you. Your instincts, reactions, feelings, angers, desires, wants, loves, and passions are in your heart and your inner being. They are not in your intellect. Your brain produces strategies for manifesting the things you want to have or to feel. First, you see your vision. Then, through believing it can happen, your brain computes the way to proceed. But to know what you wish to manifest, what is truly important, you must go to the inner caverns of your feelings, where the soul resides.

The goal of emotional fitness is to diminish the ego and drop the trappings of insecurity and competitiveness. Thus you begin to tap into your truth and what works best for you and those around you. There are two Zen proverbs I use to illustrate this point.

The first is about a couple of Zen monks who are walking along and come upon a woman at the edge of a fast flowing river. She tells them she needs to get across the river but is frightened. One of the monks offers to take her across. She thanks him and he carries her to the other side. The monk who has been watching is beside himself. He can't believe this has happened. As soon as the first monk crosses back to the other side, the waiting monk lays into him about the fact that they are monks and bound to chastity. Carrying a woman in one's arms is against all they have been taught. When the monk's tirade is finally over, the gallant monk who carried the woman across the river simply looks at the other and says, "I picked her up, carried her across the river, and put her down. It is you, my friend, who is still carrying her."

The second proverb is also about a monk, a hermit in the mountains, who is visited by an alone and frightened woman from a nearby village because she needs comfort and guidance. After a short stay with the monk, she returns to her village. A few months later, the woman discovers she is pregnant and blames the monk. When the child is born, the angry townspeople come up the mountain and deposit the child at the monk's feet, chastising him for his appalling behavior. In response to the attack the monk simply replies, "Is that so?" He then takes the child and raises it over the course of the next year. Meanwhile, the lying mother can no longer stand her guilt. She confesses that it is not the monk who was the father and that she has been protecting another all along. A very embarrassed group of people goes up the mountain and humbles themselves in apology before the monk. In response to their embarrassment, the monk looks up and again says, "Is that so?"

In both parables, the one who has clarity about the essence of his truth does not fear what others think or say. Those who have not worked out the wounds of their ego are forever inappropriate with their actions and their words. When you have peace with who you are, others cannot sway you. To the extent that you are able to let go of your stuff and clearly see yourself, you will move toward your essence and truly be.

I love great food, although I can hardly boil water. Recently I was at a dinner party and one of the guests, a competent cook, took a verbal shot at me about my lack of cooking skills. He intended to embarrass me, but because I own the fact that I am not a cook of any stature, I agreed with him and let it go. I merely said, "I am not embarrassed by what I choose not to be good at." When his jibe went nowhere, he was the one who felt embarrassed.

Only those with the courage to dismantle the ego and move into the spirit of the self will be able to enter the kingdom of their own inner and personal heaven. Here lies the wonderment of the being within, not plagued by personal insecurities and shortcomings. Once your baggage is resolved, you can embrace the essence of who you truly are. You are empowered to be in total honesty with your strengths and your limitations without blame or shame. Safe within your own heart, you are capable of forgiving and loving yourself from a place of balance and utmost respect. This is the optimum perspective from which to meet others, whether by direct word or deed or just by carrying yourself from this place of divinity, in the moment, free to move about without need for outside validation, your essence will shine.

One of the first blessings you receive from living in this new world of self acceptance is a sense of peace about not having to live up to the "should" and "should not" rules of the world. Disappointment and disapproval come from putting our power and sense of self into the hands of others. When at the mercy of prescribed roles, we are never very far away from the feeling of being less than what we "should" be. If you can let go and write your own script, anxiety and stress are minimized, secrets are abated, and the need to look over your shoulder disappears.

As my clients move onto this road, it is a joy to watch them wallow in the peace of it. The more one walks toward the light, the more one is bathed in warmth. I don't know anyone who is absolutely "there," at all times and in all ways, but it is indeed fun to meet those who are walking steadily along on their path.

The second blessing of self-acceptance is that you begin to see the world and those around you much more clearly. The feedback I get from clients is that they are struck by the many ways they notice differences in people. This is often experienced even after being in psychotherapy for only a short time. It is not uncommon that the Universe may send my adult clients on a trip to visit their parents shortly after starting our sessions. During these visits clients will notice idiosyncrasies in their families that they now realize were there all along, but it wasn't until they began to change their way of being that they were able to truly "see it." They come back to our sessions in the process of a shift. And this is just the tip of the iceberg in terms the degree to which one can create a new reality.

When the wounds of the ego begin to heal, the startling results of the healing take place automatically. Below are a few examples of the many ways I have heard these feelings described.

"I've never quite experienced people the way I do now."

"I seem to sense people better, and to know who I do and do not want to be around."

"I was sitting with some people I have known for a long time and suddenly realized how I've not been as appreciated or respected as I want to be. I realize the way my shadow wants to come out and where."

"I see how before I was at the mercy of my shadow and now I just tell it to buzz off."

The more often you take off the rose colored glasses of denial and look at yourself, the more you are able to see the true auras and intentions of those around you. I remember a long time ago, I was at a Hollywood function with a friend and he pointed out an important person in his business. I looked at the stranger, scanned him, and told my friend what I saw and what I ventured were things to be aware of when dealing with him. He looked at me in amazement and asked, "How did you do that?" I told him we all have the ability, it's just a matter of getting out of our own way so we can see with our heart (feelings) and our third eye (the metaphysical term for the area in the middle of the forehead where we get a sense of the totality of someone). This "sensing" is available to all courageous people who choose to walk through their valley of shadows and deal with themselves without distractions. It's an inside out process resulting in being in your truth, an all knowing barometer.

The more you have a feel for who you are, the more tuned in you will be to those around you. Their masks will not confuse you. As you hide less, so too will you be able to know when someone else is hiding. This is not a trick, except to those who still wear a mask. If your vision is blocked by a mask that you feel you must wear, it will not be possible to really see others. You cannot go any deeper into others than you have insight into yourself. You must remove your own mask before you are out of your way enough to see others without theirs. This is the process by which you courageously begin to walk the path of being who you are and who you are not, while taking responsibility for the ways in which you show up.

The following dialogue illustrates one of the many ways of making this work in one's life.

Client: I know I give my power away.

Dr. R.: How do you know this and how do you do it?

Client: I can see there are times at work when my boss will say something derogatory and I don't do anything about it. I want to say something, but I'm afraid I'll get into trouble.

Dr. R.: Does what your boss say have merit or is she just taking shots?

Client: A little of both I suppose. There are times when she makes comments that reflect an error in my judgment and other times she is just taking shots.

Dr. R.: The way to handle this type of situation is to first be clear about your strengths and limitations. You cannot own your power if you are not honest about who you are and who you are not.

Client: I don't understand.

Dr. R.: For example, if your boss is pointing out ways you need to improve, try to get on the same page with her. If she is being hostile there are ways of addressing her in a manner that lets her know that you do not agree with or appreciate the way she is dealing with you.

Client: That will get me fired in a hurry.

Dr. R.: Not necessarily. If there is an area you know you need to work on or she talks about an area that needs improvement then you can work with her. If what she is saying is an issue for you, then without being defensive, you can look appropriately at the improvements you need to make. You may even thank her for helping to guide you toward being a better professional. You can do this only if you are clear with yourself that you are not perfect. If you need, out of insecurity, to always be right or never criticized then you will fight this, be defensive, and resist the feedback. And, in doing this you will turn over your power to this object of perfectionism that is criticizing you and you will feel belittled and defeated. If you are able to own that you have areas that need work, then you can admit to these, work on them, and remain empowered.

Client: That sounds easier said than done.

Dr. R.: It always is. What I'm talking about it easy once you are clear about who you are and who you aren't. This is the hard work. This work allows you to stand in the face of criticism and work with it to further improve yourself. It allows you to grow and prosper rather than to fret and fight. The opposite is also true. If your boss takes a shot at you, you can stand in your truth about yourself, and from an empowered, tactful place rebuff the attack. We often get caught in an all or nothing 22." We think we either have to accept all of the criticism or explode.

Client: That is how I feel most of the time. I act like I ignore the attack because I want to keep my job, but inside I want to take her out.

Dr. R.: Exactly. Neither one of the all or nothing options offers an effective way of handling the situation. In the middle, where all balance lives, is the way to handle it. Obviously you want to keep your job and you do not want to be attacked. First, assess the validity of the attack. If the criticism does not fit, simply and from a place of truth and empowerment and without anger, let your boss know that this is not the truth. Let her know that you are open to doing things differently but that saying it to you in this way does not work for you.

Client: If I do that my boss will lose it.

Dr. R.: Obviously you know the situation better than I do. However, no one has the right to denigrate you. Therefore, no matter how you choose to do it you cannot let someone put you down. You respond tactfully, but with the resolve that there may be other ways of doing things, but you did not deserve being talked to that way. Even if you feel you cannot attend to your boss this way, it is essential that you own and know that you did not deserve that treatment and personally validate your work for yourself.

The more you venture toward your essence, the more your own direction is heightened. One might call it a "gut" sense of things, or simply your intuition. It is something you will notice when you are at a crossroads, literally or figuratively. Faced with two alternatives, you can feel which is the right way for you. There are times when you are more available to others to act out your ideal, and with increasing clarity you will begin to choose roads that were not as easy to "see" before. This is not an overnight event but an unfolding. And each turn in the road offers more foresight and wisdom.

Many people experience this type of an awakening in long-term relationships. The more they trust and let down their guard with a person, the more they are able to pick up on how someone is doing or what the relationship needs. We usually chalk this up to way it is in a good marriage." But I contend that this is the exquisite process of getting out of your own way and being able to be more in tune with another person. It is not the other person causing a new awareness, but you being more open and aware. As you move out of your intellect and into your heart and soul, you will embrace a kinesthetic sense of "knowing." You can use this process in every aspect of your life. It takes place in the realm of the spirit, where there is increasing clarity about what is right for you and the people you love.

In the case of a newly married young couple I am seeing, he is someone who wants to please in order to be liked. He agrees to go on outings when he really doesn't want to go. Sometimes he goes, but for the wrong reasons. When he shows up out of a sense of obligation, he does so with an attitude and makes everyone upset, including himself. I have worked with him and encouraged him to only go on outings when he can be truly present, and then everyone will have a good time. Of course, one would hope that a married couple could enjoy as much time together as possible. But this doesn't mean they will have everything in common or want to be together all the time. When a balance is reached, by giving each partner permission to participate or not, each will be more at peace and so will the marriage.

All divine paths are about love, acceptance, absolution, awareness, health, surrender, fullness, joy, great happiness, contentment, peace, kindness, abundance and a divine presence. We might call this Spirit, the Soul, the Universe, or the Kingdom of Heaven. This is not a contest to determine who is right. We are a collective of human beings. Spirit is the answer, not who is right about the best way to connect to Spirit.

Spirituality is the essence of every human being as well as the basis of all forms of religion, philosophy, and psychology. It is the core of our belief about how to be in the world in relation to other humans. It is even at the root of how to run a company in order for the workers' morale and therefore productivity to soar. We have so many different containers for our spirituality because the human race is very complex and diverse and different explanations work for different people. We need many ways to help us understand the Universe and our part in it so that we all can have a meaningful place of worship, a place to debate, and a point from which to get ourselves out of dysfunction. Nevertheless, all the roads lead to the same place. All the vehicles for saving our souls, minds, and hearts come back to the same well. And, there is but one well of divine guidance, forgiveness, and love. It is the same well from which we all seek answers. It is the same well from which we receive answers to the question of being.

The essence of self can be glimpsed most often when we are in the midst of meditation. We feel it right there on the horizon, where the ego of our humanness dissipates into the glow of our inner soul. The soul is our sweet spot of being. Those who have engaged in sports such as skiing, swimming, golf, dance, and the marital arts know this perfect state of balance between mind, body, and spirit. It is the fluid pattern of our being that moves within harmonic states without thought and completely outside of the realm of time. For a brief moment, we are caught so exquisitely in our passion that living on this plane ceases to exist in the presence of our soul. Many people visit this place when they make love; others know it as a creative high. Some students find it when they dive into writing or research. Time just seems to vanish. When you come out of your haze, you look around, and realize that hours you could have sworn were minutes have past.

Many people say that "time flies when you're having fun." Have you ever thought about why this is? When we are not happy it is usually because we are at the mercy of our fears and concerns. We quickly lose our path and our focus. But to follow the bliss in each moment takes the fret and fear away. Embraced by this land of the spirit, there is no hot or cold, no pain or illness, no fatigue, no hate. There is nothing but the empowered state of your sacred essence. We have all experienced glimpses of this realm of the soul. Imagine if you could let go of your learned self long enough to hang out here in this state. This is a possibility for anyone willing to walk the walk, stretch, and go the distance of being in emotional shape.

Being Human

This being human is a guest house,
Every morning a new arrival.
A joy, a depression, a meanness,
Some momentary awareness comes
As an unexpected visitor.
Welcome and entertain them all!
The dark thought, the shame, the malice,
Meet them at the door laughing,
And invite them in.
Be grateful for whoever comes,
Because each has been sent
As a guide from beyond.

—Rumi

It is critical to remember that we are beings who are here to enhance our souls by doing our inner work and learning our lessons. This requires letting go of the tag of the persona, the concern that we are important because of what we do, and the illusion that our essence is the container. We begin with knowing we are more than who we were taught to be and rediscovering our truth.

The goal is to kill the myth that we are irreplaceable. For in actuality, we are no more than the lessons we have come here to learn. Within this reality, no one is less or more valuable than the next. Imagine that your life is taking place in a very large university called the Universe. You applied here so that you could access material that will benefit your soul, graduate, and then move on. Of course, some are quicker, brighter, and more adept at certain subjects or tests than others; but until graduation, when all is tallied up and scored, no one knows who is getting the most out of the experience. And no graduate is more important a being than the next...only more learned or more serious about the lessons. No matter how well each spirit does, all will have learned what he or she either could or wanted to learn. And all will leave with the learning they came for or would allow themselves to gain before going on to the next level.

Students do not usually fear what is referred to as commencement. They look forward to achieving their goal and then moving on. What might happen instead to a student who can't tolerate the thought of finishing and graduating? The fear of each day bringing him that much closer to the "end" would be overwhelming. To what extent would this person be able to hear the lecture, take in the information, assimilate what is being taught, study, prepare, memorize, and retain and utilize what has been learned? The answer is that he would not. If this were you, wouldn't such fear take you completely off your mark, with anxiety and depression in close pursuit to devastate you? There would be no way you could achieve your purpose for entering the university in the first place. In the best-case scenario the effects would be diminished, if not wasted.

Fortunately, the fear of the "end" does not stay with us each day, and there are many times when we rise above our day-to-day fears and plug into something exciting or stimulating, at least for a while. Therefore, most students open to the bigger picture and gather up areas of essential data to help themselves along their way.

Imagine if you will that a number of university students are somehow able to experience the reality of commencement or the "end" before they have actually completed their courses. And then they are able to come back to the present and talk about this with others. These students have not just imagined going through the motions of commencement, but have truly walked with those who are already in the process of commencing. What if these students could actually hang out with souls on the other side, talk with them about their reality, and learn from them?

Now imagine that these students are able to return with all of this knowledge intact, and that no matter what fear is perceived by others, or is directed at them by others hoping to threaten or unsettle them they cannot be swayed from their newly found knowledge. They have achieved an unshakable faith that can surmount any stress, fear, anxiety, concern, or unanswered questions regarding life after commencement. In fact, when other students begin to hear about their unique experience on the other side of commencement, they want to join them in an effort to feel and know what it is they feel and know. But, as much as the earthbound students attempt to experience life after commencement, the closest they come to it is their belief or faith in this possibility. The whole demeanor of those who have come back to the present has changed. They carry themselves, attend classes, and interact differently than those around them. They carry an inner peace and serenity that can only be described as bliss. They are able to sense things and know things that before were impossible for them to know.

Next, these special students at the university begin to write down what it was they saw and learned from the graduates they had met. They do this as an inspiration to the other students, so they won't have to fret and stress about life on the other side. They say that students and teachers do not have to live the way they have been living and that there is a great deal of benefit to be witnessed in the university. When others hear what the travelers have to say, they are eager to absorb the wisdom of the messengers.

One problem however, is that many of the regular students are too preoccupied to truly observe what is going on around them. They don't understand how simple it all is and what a natural progression it is to attend the university until the end. The travelers want very much for the others to "get it," but they have to allow each student to achieve this in his or her own time and way. No one can predict who will or will not get out of the way of fear and compulsion in order to see the true nature of things.

The Hindus believe that life is an illusion and what is important is the learning, rather than any circumstance that causes the learning. The enlightened student now owns this perspective. He sees that whatever happens is just a mirror of what he has come to experience. He now knows that no matter what happens, good or bad, it is really neither good nor bad but simply more wisdom. Each experience; teacher, class, student, high, low, good, bad, reward, wound, joy, or hurt is another lesson in this short lived class called life, after which the only assets and tangible rewards one can take away are the "learned" lessons. Thus, the truth or reality of existence is to take in and absorb each opportunity, allowing the spirit to learn and grow.

One of the highest forms of learning is the illusory nature of content issues, the overt aspects of what seem to be important. On the other hand, process issues, the underlying fundamentals, are centered around what information we gather about the self. These basic concepts help to feed and teach the spirit. Those who understand this concept truly walk to the beat of a different drummer.

Our spirit chose to come to playground earth seeking information to enhance the soul. As toddlers, we are stripped of our soul memory and become the person our caregivers mold us to be. This does not mean that we are totally without remnants of our essence, but soul knowledge ceases to be our primary focus. We begin to act out with other beings the doings of our wants, insecurities, and needs in order to feel apart from whatever system has had a hold on us. As we enter the early part of our adult life, we strive to match what our peer group sees as valuable and important, typically having fun while creating a niche within the hierarchy of society. We take on what seem to be worthwhile new relationships. We live life as best we can, seeking out things we've been taught will give us some aspect of happiness.

Yet, in recent years many people have begun searching for something to feed their souls instead of their bank accounts. Society has come back to looking for a universal message as the way to reclaim one's essence and peace of mind, body, and soul.

Illusion, which the Hindus often allude to, plays out as the Universe. We do not need to become any one type of religion or belief to understand reality, but we must connect to something beyond the ego. We are here to gather the awareness we get from holding up the mirror of each day. Yet, this is still only a catalyst to a greater reality, which is our soul. What will you take with you from each day's experience? Each event reflects a soul lesson. If you run into someone who "makes" you very angry, check it out. When you have a day filled with a particular stress, check it out. Can you stop your ego from reacting and capitalize on the true purpose of this earth plane?

Those able to experience the other side and then come back again retain a certain knowing that allows them to live differently. This is not to say we should all tempt fate and try to walk to the other side and back. However, anyone can read accounts of other people's travels to other realms.

What I know is that if we embrace the fact that our time here is temporary and accept that our leaving is no more than moving on to the next center of learning, then we will be able to live joyfully in the illusion and continue to create a meaningful reality.

The following dialogue illustrates one person's longing for a deeper connection to his own soul.

Client: My profession is a lucrative one, but something is missing. I feel like my passion is not being attended to. It feels like there's a part of me that is crying out to be expressed and yet for sixty hours a week I am engaged in a left brain endeavor that is suppressing my soul.

Dr. R.: What is it you would like to be doing?

Client: I have always been an artist and I want to do more of that before I die.

Dr. R.: Most people, especially men, who have run there lives by the mentality of our materialistic society feel that as they approach midlife something is missing. This comes from the fact that the essence of self and life is quality not quantity. As we are more established and less hungry, we long for a more fulfilling life.

Client: Well, that must be it because I am really down about the way I am living. I want to expand my sense of joy and passion.

Dr. R.: There is no reason not to do this. We have to work on the ways in which you hold your identity and help you to be more in touch with your passion. You stay in your head too much and you are not sure how to tend to your heart, which is where passion lives.

Client: Okay, I'm ready. I feel so empty and alone in this. I am a sensitive man but I feel like I'm in a war zone that doesn't allow me to be vulnerable or open.

Dr. R.: To walk in this place means you have to be humble and yet know that you cannot be attacked.

Client: How is that possible?

Dr. R.: It comes from standing in your power and feelings so that you can be sensitive yet empowered. It means that you can feel what you feel and not be at risk. For instance, when you think about how much you love your wife what do you feel?

Client: I feel good. I can get hold of what she means to me and the way my heart warms as I picture her.

Dr. R.: Okay, now while you are feeling this way, if I were to call you a dirty name would you fall apart?

Client: No.

Dr. R.: Why not?

Client: Well, I just wouldn't let that happen.

Dr. R.: But, if you are vulnerable because you are feeling in your heart how much you love your wife why can't I get to you?

Client: I'm not sure. I just know that I won't let you take this good feeling away from me.

Dr. R.: Exactly. You can be in your heart and still be sensitive to your own protection or survival. This is the place of empowerment that I am talking about.

It is a place where by the very act of feeling, you are clear when an attack occurs and you have the force needed to handle it.

Client: I never thought of that before. I can see that if I own my feelings for my wife this does not mean I am vulnerable or ripe for attack. And, if I am in my truth about myself and not in my insecurities I can take care of myself.

Dr. R.: Now you got it.

11

Claiming Our Essence Within

✦

My teachings are easy to understand,
And easy to put into practice.
Yet your intellect will never grasp them,
And if you try to practice them, you'll fail.
My teachings are older than the world.
How can you grasp their meaning?
If you want to know me,
Look inside your heart.

—Lao Tzu

Illusion and Reality

Many intellectuals and scientists will tell you there is only one reality. I would agree, but what is it? Newton said the atom was like the outside of the apple peel, but Einstein blew that theory apart with $E=Mc^2$. Einstein demonstrated that the space inside the atom, at the center of it, is where the essential understanding of the atom is found. I believe that reality, true reality, may not yet have been discovered. We keep peeling away layers of the fruit in an effort to find a sweeter essence at a deeper level. These layers are like our learned personality, constantly in our way. There are very few, if any, who know the ultimate power and potential of who they are. Therefore, as you broaden and stretch the concept of who you are, so too does your reality shift to another soul level. And your experiences are constantly shifting to mirror the way you carry yourself and the ways in which you interact with others.

Those who have ventured into altered states of consciousness/ meditation challenge us as to the nature and parameters of reality. Teachers such as Deepak Chopra, Wayne Dyer, Tony Robbins, and John Gray suggest that we have only scratched the surface of our abilities. Before you heard some of their teachings, you probably thought you already knew all there was to know about reality with regard to your life, weight, financial status, and relationships. But you were mistaken.

As a society, we have a tough time dealing with the idea that we are not all knowing beings in our human state. We have this grandiosity about knowing what we can do and cannot do. Only when someone who understands that the envelope of reality may have a lot of stretching to do, and proves it, will John Q. Public change his collective opinion. Steeped in our need to stay within our personal containers of safety, we crave normalcy, even when it hurts. Thus, reality remains a mere concept because we have not yet reached the depth where true reality resides.

In the '40s, you would have been laughed at if you had talked about mankind walking on the moon. Much of what was science fiction then is scientific reality now. Those in the not so distant past thought to be madness what we accept as mainstream today. If we let go of what we believe to be so, we can move on to what could be so. Stuck in our fears and insecurities, we are never comfortable bending and stretching beyond our comfort zone. And this puts a stranglehold on our ability to touch our purer selves. Only when we allow for more can we open up to feel and experience the true nature of our being.

Some time ago, I met a Cree Medicine Man named Bear Heart. He told me a story about how one makes it snow. Probably much like you, I had a hard time believing this could be done. With doubt, we immediately put a limit on our idea of reality. But remember for a moment the first time you were told by someone important to you that you couldn't do something. And this made you want to do it even more because they said it was out of your range or impossible for you to accomplish. Remember the time you went for it and were able to accomplish it anyway? Did you not defy that person's reality? If you can remember that experience, then hold on to your own skepticism for just a moment and listen to the rest of the story.

Bear Heart told me about what he did to bring snow (and he had a clipping from the local newspaper to show he did this). He aligned himself with the oneness of nature and requested that precipitation be allowed. Mother Nature does not want to destroy her crops and so she is more than willing to help. Bear Heart's request put him in touch with that energy. Dr. Bill Little, in one of his sermons in Carmel, California, gave a metaphor that spoke to this example. He said, "Could you imagine a situation in which as a child you requested one of your parents pass the bread to you and they would not do it? It would not enter your reality for one moment that the bread would not be passed." In this same vein, if you ask the Universe to give you something with the same level of knowing, it cannot help but grant your request. The Universe, or Mother Nature, wants to do whatever it can to fulfill your expectations. The point is that you have to come with your desire resonating from the very core of your being.

You must also be absolutely sure you can handle what you claim to want. Would a truly caring parent give a child something they really did not want? If the child asked for more toys or for money, but her underlying feeling was that she didn't deserve it, do you think an all-knowing parent would give it to her? In this same manner, imagine that the Universe wants only to give you what it is you feel you deserve? What if it is not going to give you one goody more than you feel entitled to receive? Interesting concept. The reverse side of this is that, in the core of your being, when you are ready to take on some new venture, doesn't it usually show up in your life? There is an old saying, when the student is ready the teacher will appear.

Do you feel confident that you can always get a date? Do you believe that making money is easy? For many this may not be so, but for you it is. Each of us has something we know we can have in our lives, and there is very little doubt in our minds that this is so. Others may come up and ask how it is that we do what we do, or have the good fortune to have things come our way. It is because there is something in your specific nature that is in tune with how to get that certain thing, and getting it is never a problem. Therefore, the more we are able to stay out of our own way in accessing the knowing side of our heart, the more we are in touch with bringing abundance and joy into our lives.

Faith and Intention

Let the Tao be present in your life
Let it be present in your family
And your family will flourish.
Let it be present in your country
And your country will be an example
To all the countries in the world.
Let it be present in the Universe
And the Universe will sing.

—Lao Tzu

Abundance is the outpouring of the soul. From religion to psychology, we are told that the more in touch we are with the inner self, our feelings, and love, the more we are able to manifest the things we want in our lives. Abundance comes not by keeping a firm grip on life but by flowing with nature. Think about it. The more you want something the harder it seems to be to get it. But if you let things be and go on with your daily life, the object of your intention usually shows up. For example, when you want to meet someone to be intimate with, hunting and being desperate are not the ways to bring this about. But when you put out the intention and let it go, that is when the person shows up. Have you ever met someone special when you were just having fun, and not looking for or expecting it. Even more to the point, have you ever given up trying to find someone special, and then without warning, someone showed up. It is the same with material need. When we want something to show up, we must have that intention. Then let it go while staying in action toward the goal and without thinking about it every moment.

Life is a leap of faith accompanied by intentional action. First, believe that what you are asking for will come, and then release it to God and to the Universe. It does not mean you abandon your forward momentum, but do not hold the belief that you are the sole maker of your destiny. We sit in our faith, knowing that the Universal parents are unconditional in their love for us and have a grand desire to fulfill our needs. Abundance is that outpouring of love. We will get what we truly want when we understand that we deserve it.

Maybe you are saying, "Oh, I knew there was a catch. We have to know we are deserving." But, I ask you, does the child not know he is deserving of the bread? Does he have any question that the bread will appear? He may learn in a human home that the parents are not unconditional in their love for him. If this is the case he will eventually learn not to expect the bread if he is continually turned down when he asks for it. But my hypothesis is that he has to learn this. The first couple of times he asks, the child has the expectation that he is deserving of the bread and that it will be given to him. But after being turned down repeatedly the child begins to believe that he is not deserving, and so there will be no bread.

Many lose their faith as they grow up. We believe that if our god-like parents do not unconditionally want us to have abundance, and we are given the impression that we are undeserving of this abundance, it follows that we can't possibly have faith that God and the Universe will be forthcoming in abundance for us. This is the hard part of faith. This is where we have to take tangible evidence from our parents about not being deserving and put it up against an intangible Universal truth and simply believe. Like friendship, faith is tested when things are tough, not when they are easy.

We need to remember that the Universe hears us, and then continue on knowing that what we want is coming to us. This theory stems from the study of quantum physics. It states that there is a self-prophesying aspect to particles in that they react in the manner we expect of them. We also know that oneness, as espoused in Eastern philosophical texts, may be explained just as simply because we are all made up of molecules. If we could go beyond ourselves, we would be in contact with every living thing. Combining these two theories we are faced with the realization that everything, being atoms, reacts the way we want them to react in order to create our reality. Therefore, if we want something from the Universe, a Universe that is waiting to meet our expectations, then it is our own stumbling blocks that must be in the way of our receiving it all. If we could truly live with faith in a Universe that is totally connected by matter, all would be available to us. All matter responds if addressed in a way that it can understand. The essence within us is the purest of matter. And when we open our hearts we can communicate with any substance we desire.

Let's revisit the example of asking parents to pass the bread. We usually only need to ask them once, then let it go, thank those whom we've asked, and know that the bread is coming. In giving thanks, we acknowledge that we clearly expect to receive what we requested. It's a done deal. If we ask for the bread and then continue to moan about how the bread is not there and how we are lacking in bread, our parents get sick of the whining and instead focus on how impoverished we are acting. Or, our parents may forget about the original request and concentrate on giving us the disappointment we obviously expect. Your parents may even decide to give you what seems to make you feel good instead of giving you bread. If you trust the parents to want to give you the bread, then they will willingly provide you with it. The trick is not to be impatient if your parents are helping other members of the family before they help you. It may take a little longer to get the bread than you had originally expected. But instead of getting caught up in the lack of bread, give thanks and go on with your meal. Know that the bread will come, in due time.

Those who reside in the essence of the soul are clear that they are a child of the Universe, deserving of all its riches. Our forefathers knew the value of combining and balancing legal tender with the spirit. Just look at the dollar bill. On the back of it you will find an Egyptian pyramid with the symbol of the all-seeing eye, a symbol of the spiritual center located in the middle of the forehead. This kind of seeing cuts through all haze of illusion and knows what is so. Also on our American dollar is the phrase "In God We Trust," set before us as a constant reminder to keep our sight set on faith in the

Universe. Only then can we embrace abundance in the material world. The balance and honing of duality in the world underlies all abundance. What we want is increasingly available to us as we learn to live in the world of the material while never forgetting to keep our hearts open and our faith alive.

Too many of us believe that abundance is only for the fortunate, so we keep playing the lotto hoping luck will take pity on us and pay us the big bucks. We do this because we do not truly believe we are worthy of getting what we want. Every time we come from the learned personality that says, "Of course, I want more money and things in my life, but I know it can't happen," we throw in the towel and admit to further failure.

When you communicate with the Universe through intention and thank it for sending what you want and need, it will materialize. Faith is about faith, and you must hold it in a tangible way. If you do it from the ego and the personality, you will not succeed. Only when you come from the depths of your belief and truth will the Universe know you are sincere. If I give my dog a command in a whisper that lacks conviction he will most likely ignore me. But if I state my intention and expect that my dog will do what I say, I get much better results. The same is true in raising children. If you ask a child to go to bed in a passive voice that lacks conviction, what usually happens? It is only when you say what you want from a place of sincere conviction that you get results. The Universe reacts in the same way, responding with abundance to the core of your being as your soul unites with your truth and not one moment sooner.